W9-BMX-301

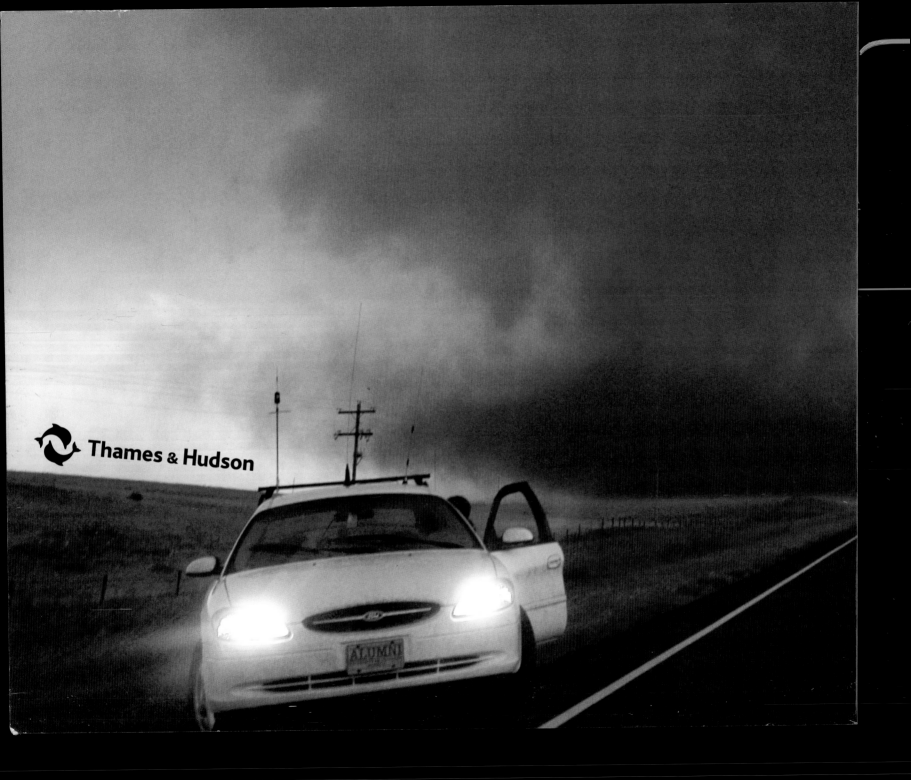

Thames & Hudson

ADVENTURES IN TORNADO ALLEY THE STORM CHASERS

Mike **Hollingshead** and **Eric Nguyen**
Introduction by **Chuck Doswell**

with 340 color illustrations

Eric Nguyen passed away in September 2007. The contents
of this book represent the best of Eric's work, and Eric's work
was his life, chasing storms and tornadoes across the Great Plains.
He was taken from his family and friends much too young, but he
will always journey with us under the big skies of Tornado Alley.

Amos Magliocco

Edited by Ruby Quince

Adventures in Tornado Alley

© 2008 Mike Hollingshead and Eric Nguyen

Introduction and The Science of Storms
© 2008 Thames & Hudson Ltd, London

All Rights Reserved. No part of this publication may be
reproduced or transmitted in any form or by any means,
electronic or mechanical, including photocopy, recording
or any other information storage and retrieval system,
without prior permission in writing from the publisher.

First published in paperback in 2008 in the
United States of America by Thames & Hudson Inc.,
500 Fifth Avenue, New York, New York 10110

thamesandhudsonusa.com

Library of Congress Catalog Card Number 2007906880

ISBN 978-0-500-28737-8

Printed and bound in China by C&C Offset Printing Co. Ltd

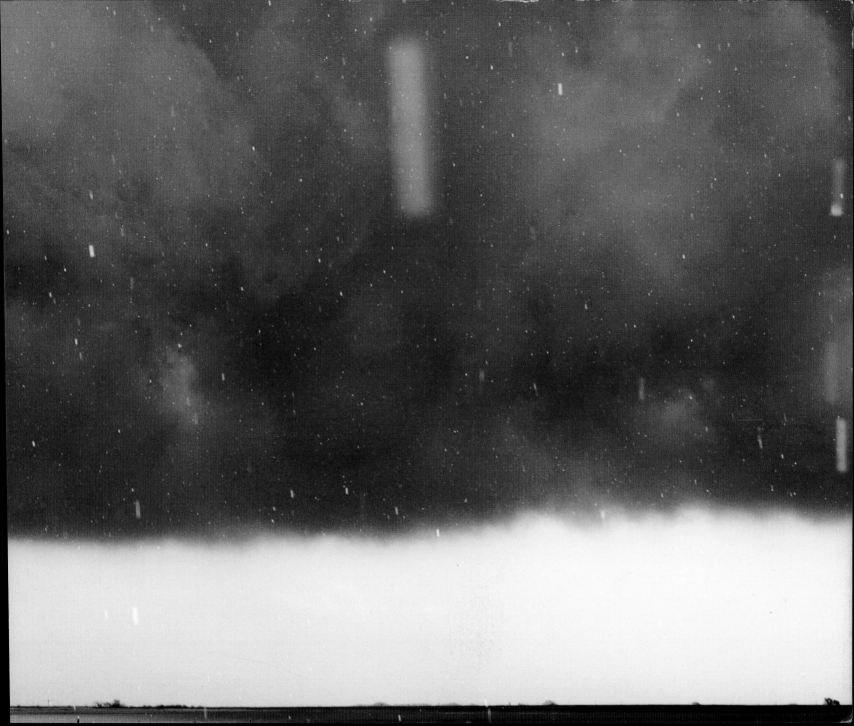

CONTENTS

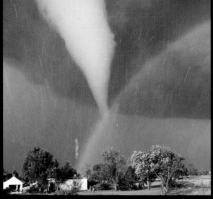
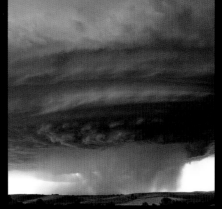
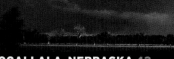
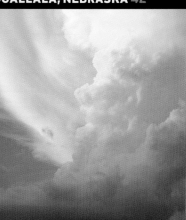

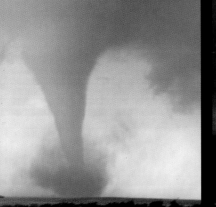
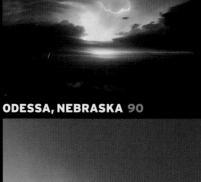
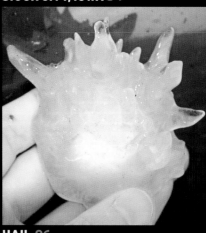

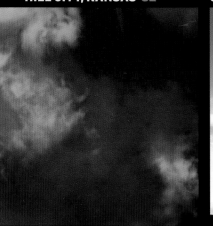
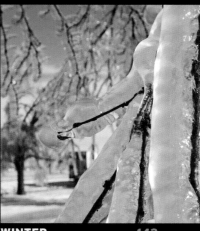
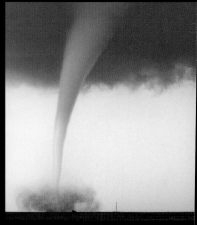

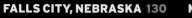

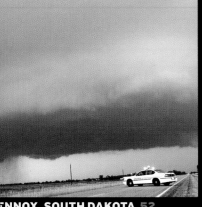
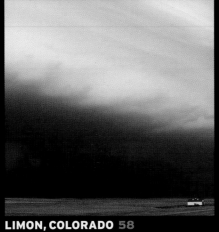
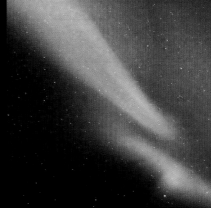
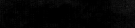
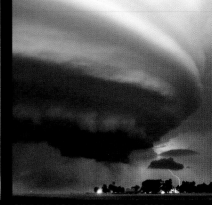

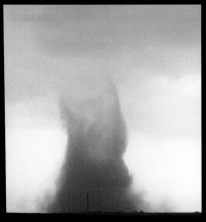
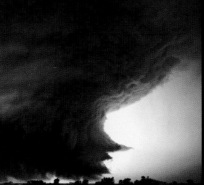
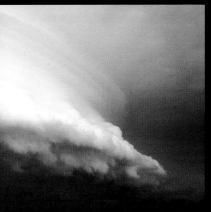
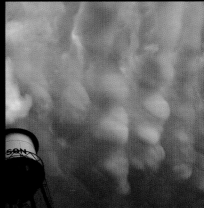

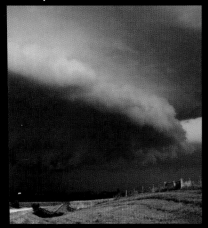
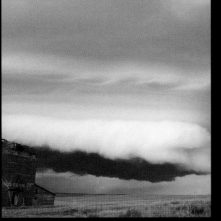
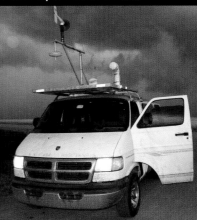

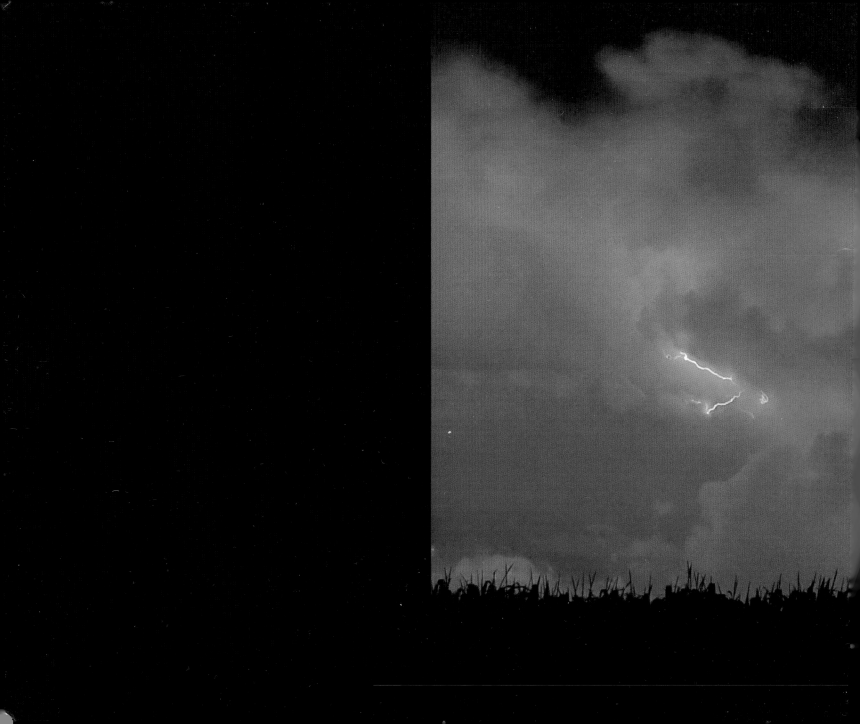

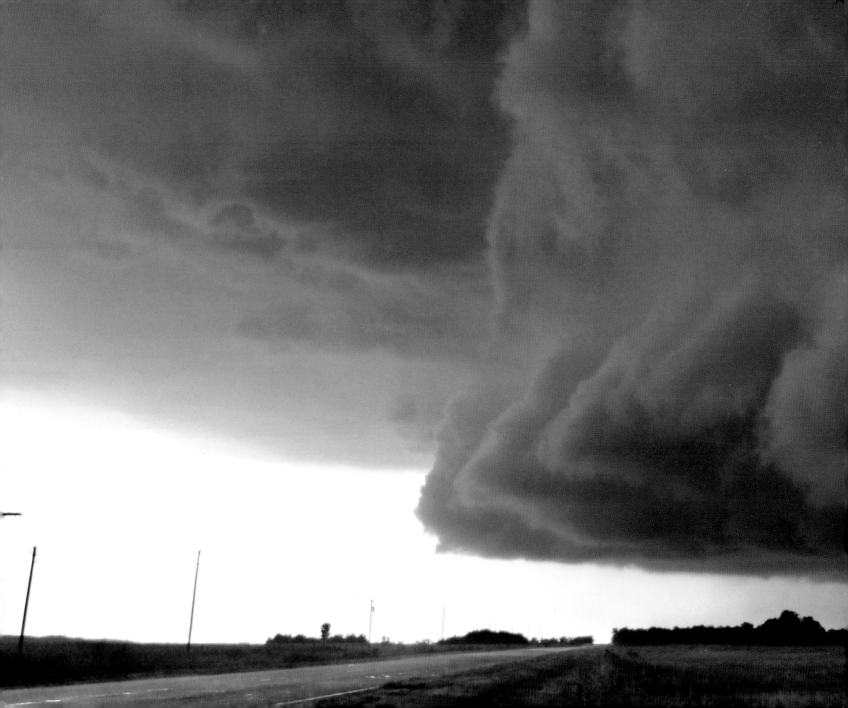

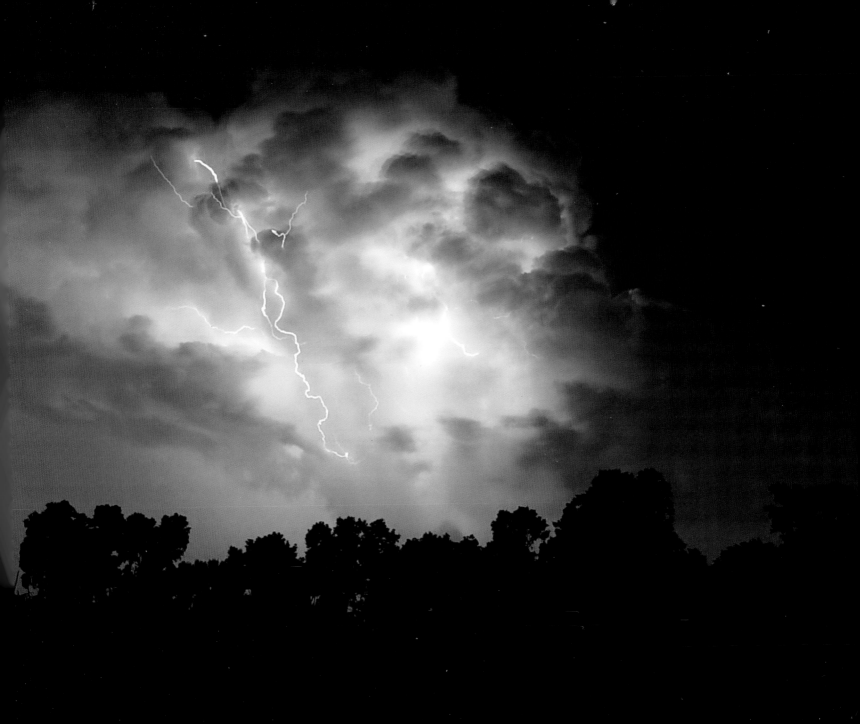

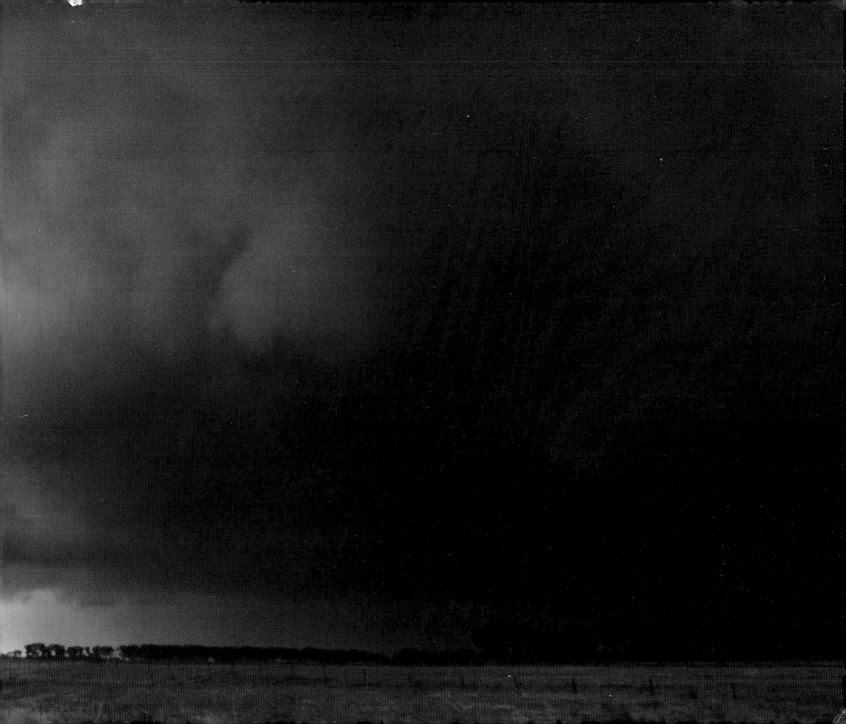

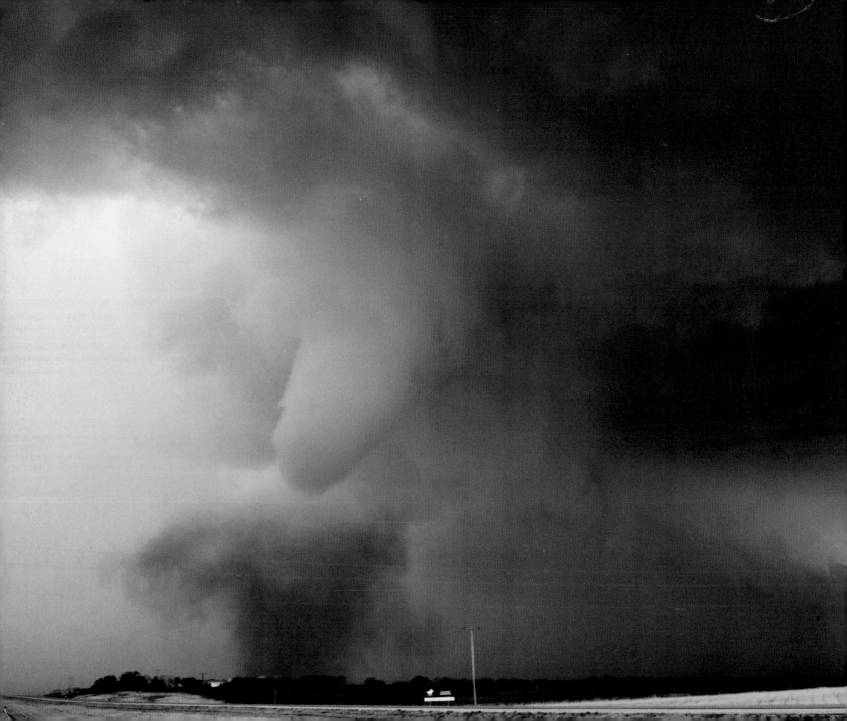

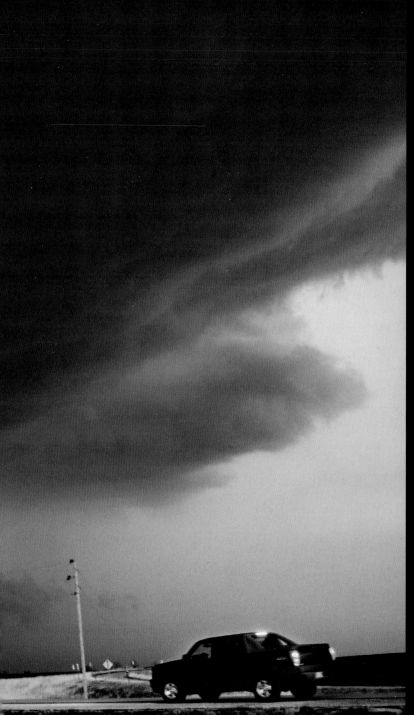

PREFACE

Spanning the whole of the American mid-west, *Adventures in Tornado Alley* collects some of the most visually arresting extreme weather scenery witnessed in the early stages of the careers of two of the most exciting photographers on the scene. Eric Nguyen and Mike Hollingshead have won audiences worldwide with their captivating photo diaries of their time in pursuit of these majestic and sometimes destructive storms. Combining an obsessive passion for storm science and forecasting with a knack for capturing the unpredictable and rare shapes thrown up by the weather systems, our narrators scour the countryside, from spring to the fall, in search of that perfect scene, sometimes crossing paths, but invariably focused on their solitary goal and personal experience in the midst of a super-storm.

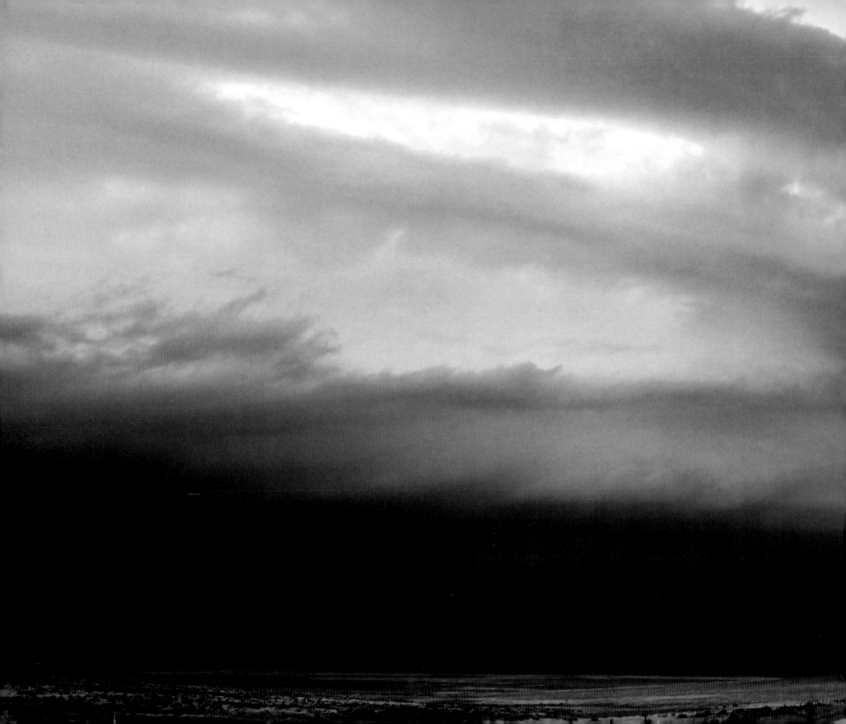

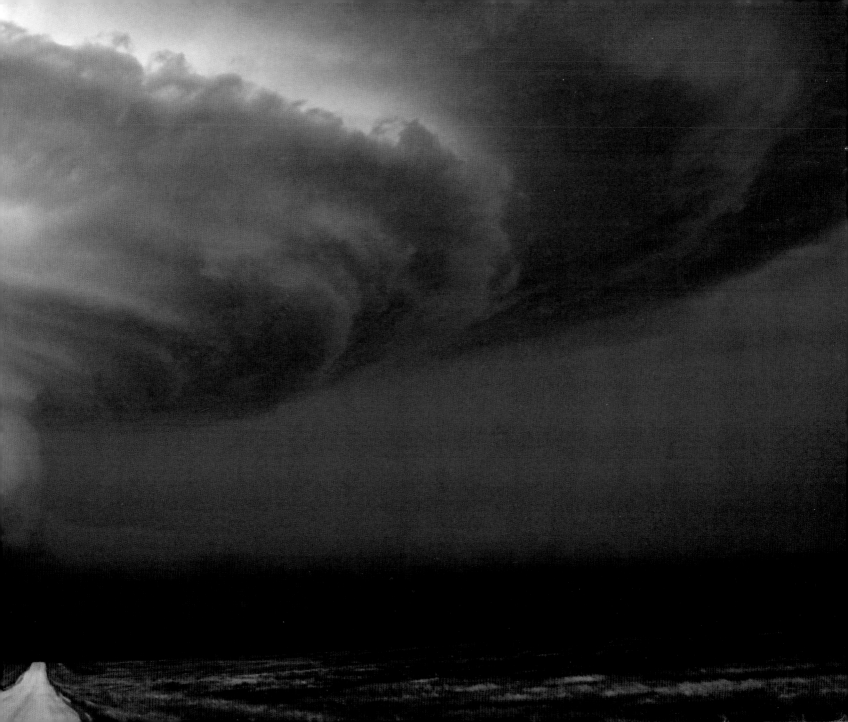

INTRODUCTION

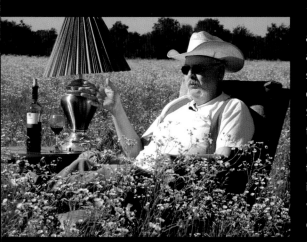

Mike Hollingshead and Eric Nguyen weren't yet born when I did my first serious storm chase, on April 18, 1972. Storm chasing has become far more common since then. Mike and Eric are leading members of a new generation of serious storm chasers.

No one knows who the first storm chaser was, but I know that David Hoadley and Roger Jensen were storm chasing as far back as the mid-1950s. They remained largely anonymous for many years. When we began chasing in the early 1970s, therefore, we had to learn it on our own, and we did so under the banner of a scientific project called the Tornado Intercept Project, run jointly by the National Severe Storms Laboratory in Norman, Oklahoma, and the University of Oklahoma, where I was then a graduate student.

There are as many reasons to chase as there are chasers, but for most, a primary goal is to see a tornado. Chasers range from scientists doing storm chasing as part of a formal scientific study of tornadoes, to serious hobbyists, to raw beginners. Some storm chase only for science, some do it for the chance to see powerful storms, some do it for the attention they get by being members of a group that many people feel is rather crazy, and some do it for the money they can get for their photos and video. Although it is possible to earn money storm chasing, there are virtually no *professional* storm chasers. Almost all storm chasers do so as a hobby, not a job. Income from video and still images isn't likely to sustain a chaser year around (unless living a *very* Spartan life style), and even those paid to chase for TV stations during storm season clearly must have some other way to support themselves outside the stormy time of the year.

Most chasers are *not* seeking an adrenaline rush by putting themselves in serious danger. The excitement is *not* the prospect of imminent death – it is the chance to witness a spectacular atmospheric event that few will ever see. Tornadoes are rare in any one place, usually last only a few minutes, and for the most part can't be seen even by people within a few miles. Using some basic common sense, storm chasing isn't all that dangerous, but clearly the potential for danger is always present. A single reckless or careless act can put the chaser at risk, and can endanger others beside the chaser. The main risk is not from storms, though. It is the danger we all face simply by driving on the roads. Considerable anxiety is present when chasing: will we arrive in time, will the storm produce a tornado? This urgency can lead to risky behavior on the roads, often slick with rain. The temptation to drive too fast or take chances is strong when storm chasing.

Lightning is the next most dangerous element of risk – several chasers have been struck. After that are the dangers posed by a tornadic storm: the tornado itself, the non-tornadic "straight" winds, the hail, and the heavy rain. Fortunately, to my knowledge, no chaser has ever been killed or seriously injured by the storm itself. But the risks are clearly there, so this is not a hobby to be undertaken casually.

Part of the fun of chasing is the challenge of forecasting when and where tornadoes are most likely. This is an important skill and even non-meteorologists can become reasonably adept at this difficult task. You have to be quite close to a developing storm to have any chance of manoeuvring into a position where you can see any tornado it might produce. In order to understand storms and the weather processes that produce them it helps to be a meteorologist, although it is not absolutely necessary. Once storms begin, knowing which storm to chase is never an easy decision. Storms are moving targets, in general, and a single bad road choice can cause the whole chase to fail. Bad road choices are remarkably easy to make! The storm itself can dictate which roads to avoid because driving into the part of a storm where large hail is falling is a good way to lose your windshield and end your chase day. Unfortunately for chasers, road options in some parts of the plains are quite limited so it is easy to find yourself shut out of a position from which to see the action of a storm.

From the beginning, it was clear to me that storm chasers span a wide range of personalities and have very different views about how chasing should be done. Responsible storm chasers (the majority) report what they see happening to the National Weather Service (NOAA) or to local storm-spotter networks so that warnings about the storm can spread to the population at risk from the storm. These responsible chasers share their photos and video freely with scientists and those who study storm spotting around the nation. Unfortunately, with any large group, there are always a few who are not responsible – they take unnecessary chances and put others at risk in their efforts to get to a tornado. Irresponsible storm chasers never report what they see and refuse to share the fruits of their chase experience with anyone except perhaps the public media, to draw attention to themselves. For a few, as my long-time friend and chaser Gene Moore has said, "It's not about the storms for these guys. It's about *them*!"

I first heard about Mike and Eric a few years back, and when I began to see their images online, I was immediately struck by how good their photographic skills were. From my experience, anyone can get lucky and capture a spectacular shot, but what I began to see from both Mike and Eric was that chase after

chase, they both had a real knack for being in the right place at the right time. Obviously, they have gained the knowledge and mastered the art of chase forecasting, they consistently make good chase decisions, and they seem to know how to be in position for the spectacular shot. In my experience, this capability is never just a series of lucky accidents. These two are really *good*! Of course, in chasing, no one ever sees everything every time, and all of us wind up "busted" on after making a bad decision or chasing on a day with little or nothing worth going after. This failure is inevitable and is, in fact, the most common outcome of any chase. It is never easy to see a tornado.

It is evident to me also that Mike and Eric are *responsible* chasers, so I know that their work is going to reflect credit on us all. As a long-time chaser, I've been pleased to welcome them into the loosely knit community of storm chasers. Most chasers are aggressively individualistic. Chasers usually don't much care for working in teams unless they're part of a scientific project. I've chased several of the same storms as Mike and Eric without ever seeing them on the road. Even though other chasers are likely to be around, being alone with your chase partner during a spectacular storm event on the plains is a sublime moment. I know I prefer that to being part of a crowd of chasers – called a "chaser convergence." Even though I'm always pleased to encounter friends, chasers like to savor the experience on their own.

New technologies, such as live radar data on your laptop computer as you go down the road, have made chasing much easier than it was when I began to do it, but it isn't easy even with that technology. I notice that in most circumstances when I *do* see other chasers in the right place at the right time, it is still mostly the seasoned veterans, with or without the fancy new gadgets.

Mike and Eric seem to have taken the art of storm photography to new heights with their images in terms of the subject matter, the composition, the exposures, the sharpness – all hallmarks of outstanding photographers. They obviously both share my excitement over aspects of the storm other than just the tornado. Many of the photographs in this book are not of tornadoes, but nevertheless they have produced images that speak eloquently about the grandeur and beauty of storms that many people will never see for themselves. In storm chasing, you have the chance to see a pageant of power and elegant form unfold before your eyes, even in the absence of the ultimate: a tornado. Mike and Eric have captured that over and over in these images.

DR. CHARLES A. (CHUCK) DOSWELL
NORMAN, OKLAHOMA

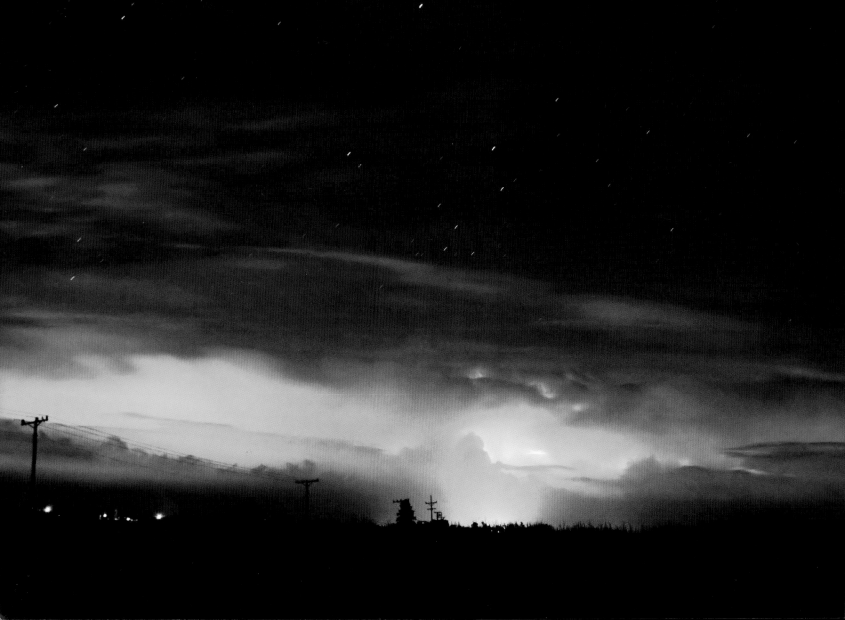

THE AUTHORS

MIKE HOLLINGSHEAD

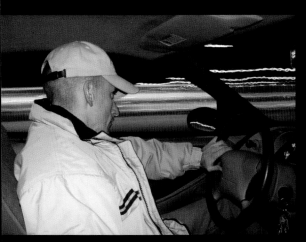

It's hard for me to step back and see how crazy chasing storms is. I'll wake up early and drive more than six hundred miles from home in Nebraska to Texas, all for nothing. The odds are stacked against me seeing anything, but the majority of the time I'll jump into my car and drive to another state at the slightest hint of a storm because I'm afraid that I'll miss something if I don't.

I was born in Blair, Nebraska, in March 1976 and I've lived here all my life. As a kid I would stay up at night during a thunderstorm and watch lightning until I couldn't keep my eyes open anymore. I would make my father drive to the top of a hill when a storm was approaching. One of us (mostly me) would get scared and we'd head back down the hill, but as I got older he was the one sitting in the car, wanting to go back. Then came hours of watching mail-order

tornado videos, which became an obsession, and all I wanted to do was see a tornado in action. When I got my driver's licence it meant I could really get out there, so I'd keep an eye on the weather forecasts and head off for the hills around Blair to watch any storms that were approaching, but I never got to see a tornado in those early days.

Around the winter of 1998 I started to consider going out further and actually chasing storms. For whatever reason I never managed to do so that year. In 1999 I was working for a maintenance contractor at the massive Cargill plant in town, but it was hard to get time off for chasing. I remember on April 8 that year I was aware of a tornado event that was about to happen in Iowa and I really wanted to chase, but I couldn't get out of work and it drove me crazy. About a month later, on a Sunday when I wasn't working, two tornadic supercells blew over Nebraska – one about thirty miles north of town and one a couple of counties south – so I just grabbed some maps and headed out for my first real chase. Before long, I could see that it really was going to tornado and I was flipping out in anticipation. You can't beat the feeling of catching your first tornado, but seeing one on your first chase is like winning the lottery on your first go! It was all wrapped in rain and I could barely make it out, but once I'd seen it, I knew I was totally hooked.

Normally when you're chasing you never really see the damage because you're staying in front of the storm all of the time to be able to get a clear view, but on this first chase I wasn't yet always on top of it

and trying to catch it I passed an overturned semi trailer in a field and lots of chewed up trees, which made the destruction I'd seen in the videos that much more real. After seeing the tornado and the damage, the traffic was stopped by a cop who rerouted us to a new road and put me right in front of a new forming tornado. Feeling a little panicky, I ended up taking shelter in a flimsy tin-walled gas station building with a bunch of nervous locals, with the power out and tennis ball-sized hail battering us for 30 minutes, while the radio repeatedly told us a huge tornado was heading for us and to find a basement. It was a scary experience, but I was on a high for days afterward and I guess from that point I was a chaser.

During the next year of chasing I realized I'd have to learn how to forecast if I was going to catch tornadoes, and ever since I've spent time reading and researching, picking up stuff along the way, but being out there really is where you learn the most. I didn't have plans or a desire to shoot still images of the storms when I started, I just video taped them on a cheap camcorder for my own records, but I started to see such cool skies that I needed something better to show on my website, so in 2002 I bought my first stills camera: a Sony F707. It was a big deal for me at the time because it wasn't cheap, but it was a good investment.

Tearing off after storms straight from work and at weekends began to be a real pain and by 2004 my job was getting in the way of storms and I came to hate it, so I quit. I didn't have a plan other than to chase for the spring and summer and then get a job in the fall when I ran out of money. I was almost forced to get a job again in November, but I got some shots of auroras (see page 66) that exploded on the internet and saved my self-employment. Three years later and I still haven't gotten a job outside of chasing and I'm hoping it's going to stay that way. I never really considered myself a photographer, but it's how I earn my living now.

Each year I increased the amount of chasing and by 2006 I was doing about 40 chases a year and over 20,000 chase miles. People forget that when you're chasing most of your time is spent on the road getting to targets or waiting for things to happen and the majority of chases are a "bust" where you end up with nothing worth shooting, or even worse, a "clear sky bust," where you really have nothing. It can be depressing when you've been in the seat of a car for twelve hours, extremely tired, pissed off that you've chased crap storms, and you're facing a long drive home. But as much as I can be pissed off on a bust, or even a whole year of busts, which is how it felt in 2006, I know I can't do without it – I'm totally addicted.

My work covers all sorts of weather conditions, so sometimes I'll go to shoot specific things such as lighting or auroras (see page 66), but the majority of the time I'm in pursuit of powerful storms. The main goal is to find great structure to capture, but storms are so varied and each one is unique so any element might become the focus of the storm. I guess I'm just looking for craziness of any form – crazy structure, mutant hail, insane tornadoes.

There's also the experience of being battered by a storm or near to a tornado, which brings some of the real highs of chasing.

People have been chasing since way before birth of the internet, but it has a huge impact on what we do, beyond being able to access live forecasting information. Chasing has exploded because most chasers share their images over the net, giving people all over the world a chance to enjoy these rare events that relatively few of us get to see, meaning more people are attracted to the hobby. Sometimes a set of images will get picked up on email chains and life becomes crazy for a few weeks. I feel like my inbox is going to burst into flames with all the questions I get from my website (extremeinstability.com) and I kind of want to hide away from it all. Incidentally, probably the most common question is about how close I've been to a tornado, so in case you're wondering, the closest I've come to a tornado (only once) is an eighth of a mile for sure and less than a mile quite frequently. The largest I've seen was probably June 9, 2003 in O'Neill, Nebraska, which had a damage path a third of a mile wide and the July 12, 2004 tornado in Bartlett, Nebraska (see page 120), which must have been a quarter of a mile wide. The strongest was near Hill City, Kansas, on June 9, 2005 (see page 82), which had near violent motions in it, at least early in its life.

People assume that chasing is a high-risk activity, but by applying a little common sense, this couldn't be further from the truth and you'd have to go out

of your way for it to pose a threat. Even 100 mph wind won't turn your car over, but it will knock big trees over and kill you in a hurry, so be careful not to stand or park near anything that might be cause for concern. Tornadoes are so rare that you'll have a hard time finding one that will hurt you, and add that to the fact that they are only covering one spot of land – normally a relatively small one and for a short period of time – the chance of being in that spot is extremely slim. Lightning is the thing that scares me the most, but the risk is easy to minimize. If lightning is striking nearby, do yourself a big favor and just stay in the car and you'll most probably be fine. It might sound goofy, but I don't think of this hobby as dangerous at all – a deer coming through my windshield while driving home at night scares me much more than anything a storm will throw at me. At least this is how I feel after doing this a while. I certainly thought the opposite when I started chasing or was just watching storms.

I always chase alone and I'm pretty sure I always will. People ask if they can ride along or if I need a chase partner, but I always refuse. I only want to worry about myself, go as close, or stay as long as I want. I want to be the only reason I have to stop. I'll go out of my way to avoid meeting up and caravanning – even when I do meet with a few chasers I know fairly well – because I'll stay in one spot for too long, talking away, and miss stuff. That said, I'm not too much of a jerk, so if you do see a black Mustang with Nebraska tags parked near a storm don't be afraid to stop and say hello.

ERIC NGUYEN

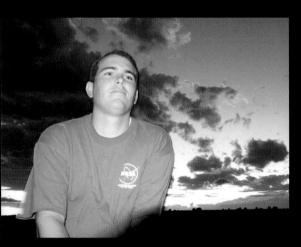

By the time my parents picked me up at about 4.30 am, I was explaining to them that maybe chasing was a bad idea for me.

My first recollection of an actual storm was when I was around seven years old: my sister was terrified and ran for shelter, but I was mesmerized and wanted to watch. I remember looking up storms in an old 1960s encyclopaedia we had in the house and feeling this urge to learn more, and pretty soon I was always in the library, soaking up as much as I could about storms. The internet opened the door to new realms of information, so I just kept on reading and watching, and by 1999 I went to study meteorology at the University of Oklahoma. I guess I've been learning about the weather pretty much all of my life.

I started chasing properly in 1994 when I was 16, but I did a lousy job of it. I remember once when I was 17 and the tornado warning sirens went off in the town I lived in (Keller, Texas); I got a call from my mom telling me to get home quickly, but I stayed out and spent a couple of hours chasing around trying to find the tornado. I really didn't know what I was doing so I didn't catch anything, and thankfully my mom didn't mind too much. It took a couple of years to find the money and time to go out further, and it wasn't until around 1997 that I felt like I knew what I was looking for and where to find it.

In those early days I used to chase alone with just a map, a scanner, and a camera. For me, chasing is all about experience, making your own forecasts and your own decisions is the best way to learn. Of course, storms are unpredictable and even with all the latest information it's easy to get it wrong, but my experience has given me a good sense of how to stay on top of a storm.

I'll chase the whole strip of territory from central Texas up to the Dakotas, east of the Rockies, west of the heavy tree line from southeast Oklahoma and up to eastern Minnesota. Ideally, I'm looking for areas with decent roads, no trees or much local traffic, which, thankfully, pretty much characterizes most of the landscape in the plains. I'm a structure chaser and adore the slow-moving supercells with gorgeous composition as they crawl along the high plains. Watching these huge, powerful beasts approach is unlike anything I'll ever experience in my life, and I'll never get tired of it.

I love the mixture of butterflies and excitement in the morning when you know you can get away to chase, the day is looking good for storms and you're glued to the computer, trying to decide when and where to go. There are so many times since then when I've been consumed by my love of storms: the back-to-back tornadic storms throughout May 2004 were a rollercoaster of fun that I'll never forget (see page 144), but if I had to pick one, the incredible tornado at Mulvane, Kansas, on June 12 that year (see page 26) was the real highlight of what I've seen so far. I'm still in awe of that storm every time I see pictures of that day.

However much you know, sometimes you're just plain beaten by a storm. Early on in my chase career one storm had me thinking I might not chase again. It was a very windy day, and two explosive towers had gone up in western Texas in May 1998. I got out of the car to get some pictures and a powerful gust blew the door closed, locking me out. Argh! It took brand new car, but at least I was back on the chase. For the rest of the day I was trying to avoid baseball-sized hail and driving underneath wallclouds. Then, late that night, a bolt of lightning struck the car, frying my ham radio and blowing out all the electrics. I was stuck out on some rural road in the middle of the night for five hours until a tow truck finally came to take me to the nearest town at 3 am. By the time my parents picked me up at about 4.30 am, I was explaining to them that maybe chasing was a bad idea for me. They both said that these things can happen in life and I would bounce back. It didn't take long as I was frantically trying to rent a car the next morning to chase later that day.

Originally, I would try to shoot video and photographic stills, but I eventually found photographs far more rewarding. In 2003 I upgraded to a digital SLR camera, which meant I had a lot more freedom to shoot as much as I wanted. My pictures have been featured in all sorts of magazines and books, and I love to share my chases with readers of my website (www.mesoscale.ws).

Along the way I've gotten to know other chasers who I'll run into and chase with, and all the little adventures we have and the funny things that happen are what really makes each chase day special. When the sky settles for the night, we usually stop at the same places to share the enjoyment of what we've seen.

and chase full time. Luckily, my work is pretty cool with what I do, so I can get the time off or swap with someone, giving me the opportunity to chase a lot. I encourage my kids to explore math and science, and I suppose they are more aware of storms than most. If they choose to take the same path I have, then I'll be just as accepting as my parents were.

All the little adventures we have and the funny things that happen are what really makes each chase day special.

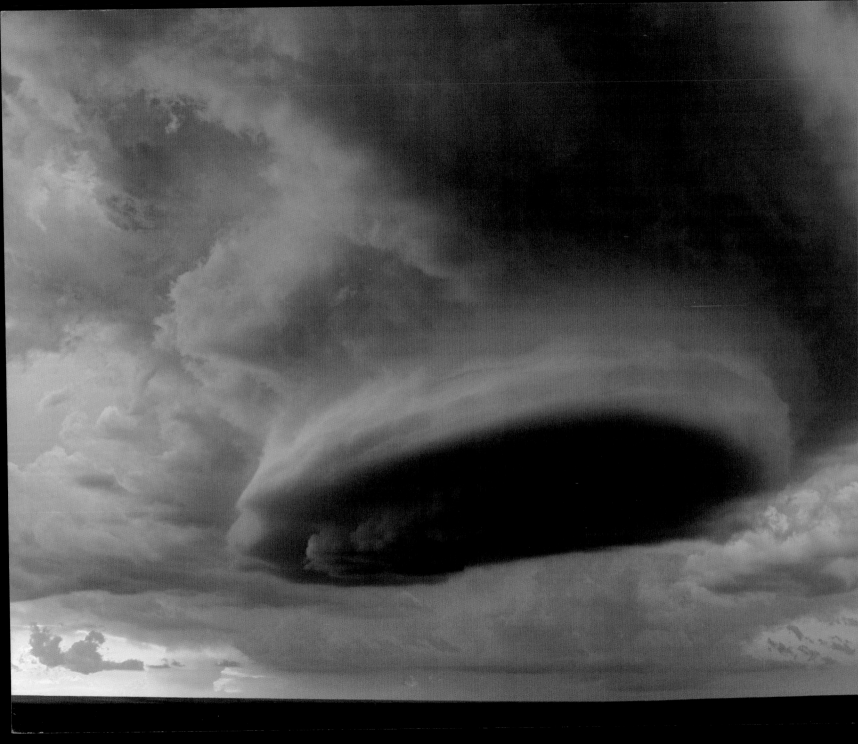

In storm chasing, you have the chance to see a pageant of power and elegant form unfold before your eyes, even in the absence of the ultimate: a tornado.

As it turned out, it was a good gamble because I had probably the greatest chase of my life!

MULVANE, KANSAS
June 12

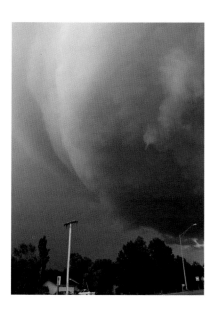

ERIC: I'd missed out on a major storm outbreak a few days earlier because I had to prepare for a conference, and I felt like I needed a decent chase to make up for it. Most chase days you find something pretty mediocre, so missing an event forecast well in advance, as I had, is twice as annoying. I made plans for a chase on this day with a chaser friend, Scott Currens, and gambled on the best target we could reach. As it turned out, it was a good gamble because I had probably the greatest chase of my life!

We get to McPherson, but the storm isn't so great and gradually dissipates, leaving us little time to regroup. As we're preparing to head home with nothing to show for the day, we hear about storms firing 70 miles south of us: an hour's drive. Perhaps normally we'd cut our losses, but today we're desperate and head toward Wichita.

On the way down we hear about a tornado striking west of the interstate. We can see storms developing along a new outflow boundary from a complex of thunderstorms, and a magnificent rotating updraft. Everything seems to be slotting into place, and judging by the violently rotating base of the cloud it seems we've caught it just in time.

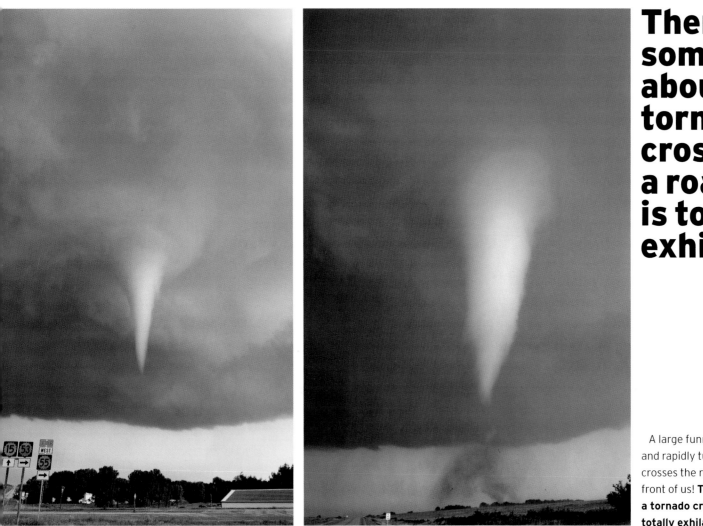

There's something about a tornado crossing a road that is totally exhilarating.

A large funnel sprouts from the base and rapidly turns into a tornado that crosses the road about 100 meters in front of us! **There's something about a tornado crossing a road that is totally exhilarating** – it's like crossing your path with a perfect view.

The storm looks too high-based to produce tornadoes that might touch down, but **it's a pretty determined storm**. The tornado fully condenses to the ground and **kicks debris as it uproots trees in the distance.**

The tornado hits a metal building, spinning up aluminium and steel debris like glitter falling from cloud. Added to the rainbow in the foreground it makes a stunning scene. The funnel hovers over a care center, but thankfully doesn't get close enough to do any damage.

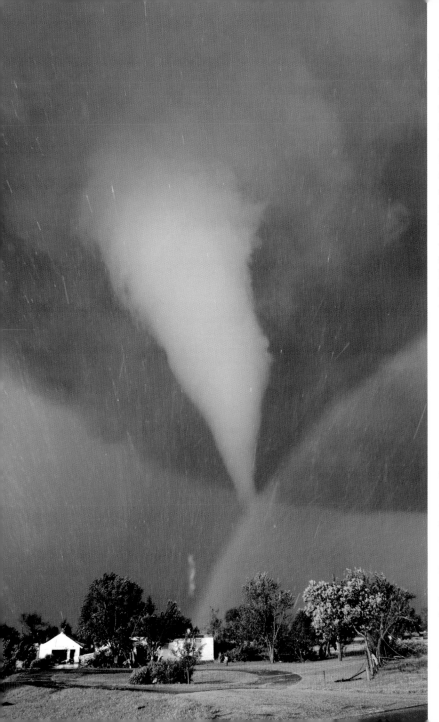

Hail starts to hit and the tornado strengthens and knocks down power lines near the road. Luckily, we're able to drive over them and continue south to observe the tornado from the west. Typically, this is a poor position as rain can wrap around the funnel, obscuring the view, but this one stays relatively dry and we can see the whole thing. **A few chasers have windows shattered by softball-sized hail** (about 4.5 inches [11.5 cm] in diameter), but we manage to avoid it.

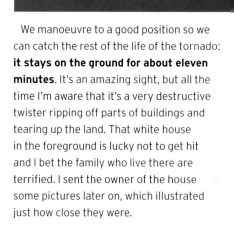

That white house in the foreground is lucky not to get hit and I bet the family who live there are terrified.

We manoeuvre to a good position so we can catch the rest of the life of the tornado: **it stays on the ground for about eleven minutes**. It's an amazing sight, but all the time I'm aware that it's a very destructive twister ripping off parts of buildings and tearing up the land. That white house in the foreground is lucky not to get hit and I bet the family who live there are terrified. I sent the owner of the house some pictures later on, which illustrated just how close they were.

It's an amazing sight, but all the time I'm aware that it's a very destructive twister ripping off parts of buildings and tearing up the land.

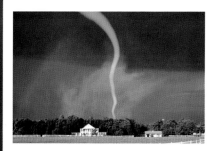

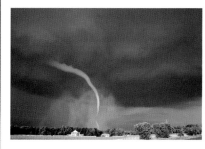

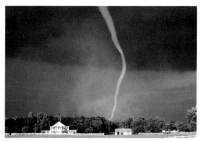

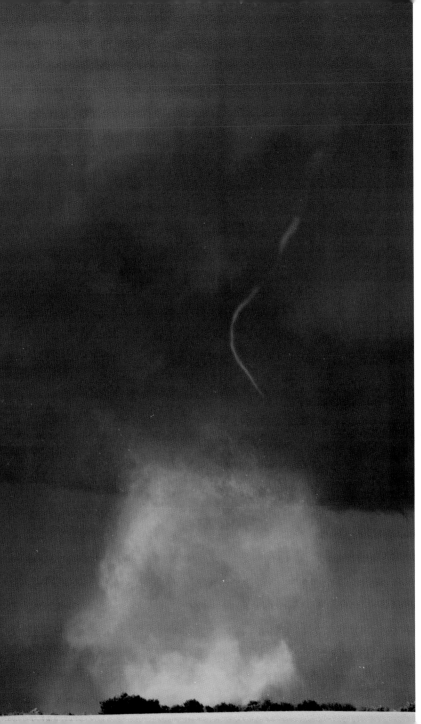

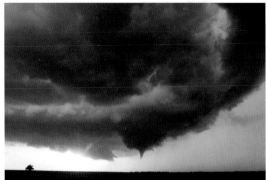

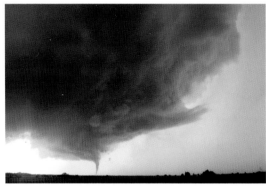

Almost as quickly as the tornado had come, it weakens and disappears in a strange way, with no visible sign of a complete occlusion. It just seems to vanish rapidly for no reason, **leaving small pieces of debris to fall from the sky for another ten minutes or so.**

The circulation of the storm moves southward on our radar data, without producing another funnel until about 30 minutes later, when the leading edge of the outflow catches up with the storm and creates a new tornado against the backdrop of the setting sun. It's a pretty weak tornado and we gradually lose the detail of the storm in the darkness, **but it's a great scene to close the day**. Who needs Iowa when you catch tornadoes like that!

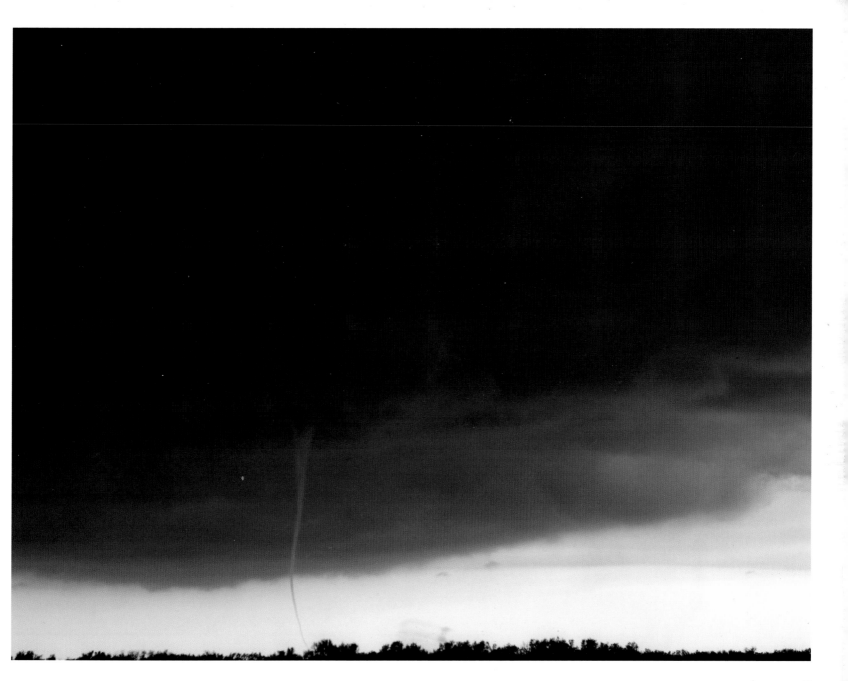

To think I could have sat out a show this good that was right on my door step!

SIOUX CITY, IOWA
May 28

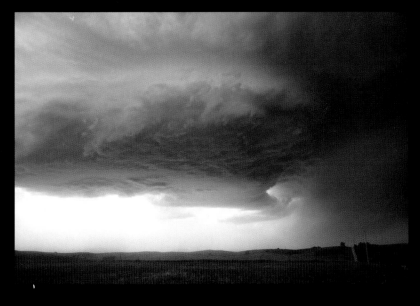

MIKE: I almost didn't chase this day because it didn't look so great. I had been checking out the data online and there was nice directional shear, but it wasn't very strong, so I figured it wasn't worth the drive. Thankfully, Steve Peterson convinced me to check it out and I'm sure as hell glad I did. To think I could have sat out a show this good that was right on my door step! We headed out to Spencer, Nebraska.

After some work it starts to crank...and boy does it crank. It now has raging inflow that is probably 40 mph and my eyes are quickly full of dirt.

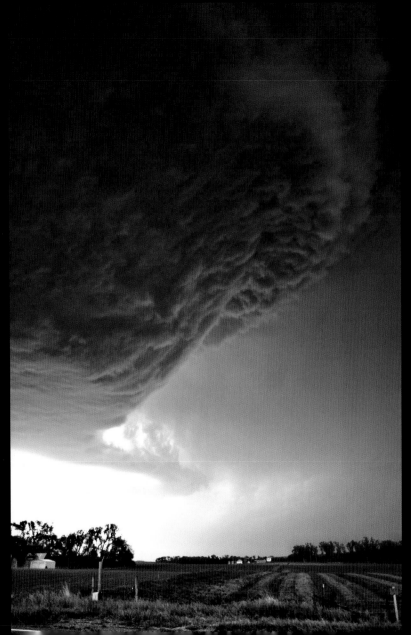

it keeps picking up in strength
and I'm keeping close to it: Steve
has moved east and calls me
to ask if I've seen the amazing
structure. I move east, see this,
and get a whole lot more excited
about the day's prospects.
**It's got to be one of the coolest
scenes I've seen while chasing
and it is about to get a whole
lot better.**

I don't get how anyone can drive under this and not feel the need to pull over and watch.

I've never seen anything quite like this.
**The storm is sucking inflow in extremely
hard and creating some crazy structures.**
Note how smooth the cloud base is away
from the center – the speed of the inflow
being sucked into that base must be
incredible. The downdraft of rain to the
side of it has an unbelievably sharp cut-off!
I bet you could almost jump in and out of
the core...dry...wet...dry...wet...I don't get
how anyone can drive under this and
not feel the need to pull over and watch

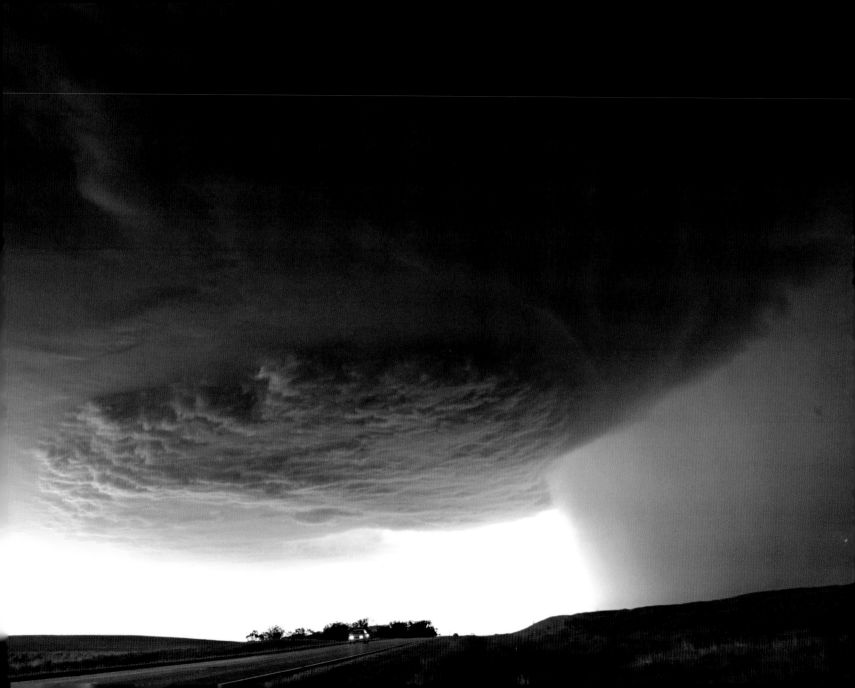

It looks like a structure-only storm (no real chance of tornadoes), so we keep our distance to make sure we get the best of it. An arm of the storm swings around and feeds back west into it, creating a big coil. You can see a little sculpted lowering at the base and **it looks like it might produce a tornado, but it doesn't**. Still, I'm not disappointed with a storm this great!

Still, I'm not disappointed with a storm this great!

Independence Day II, here we come!

The winds are getting stronger and stronger, ripping west into the storm while the power lines overhead scream as the gusts blow through them.

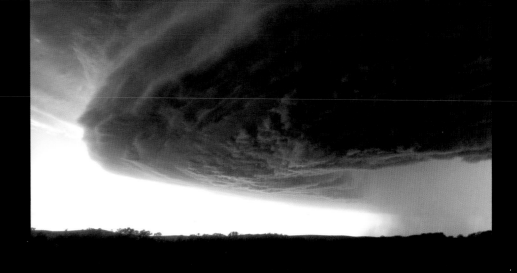

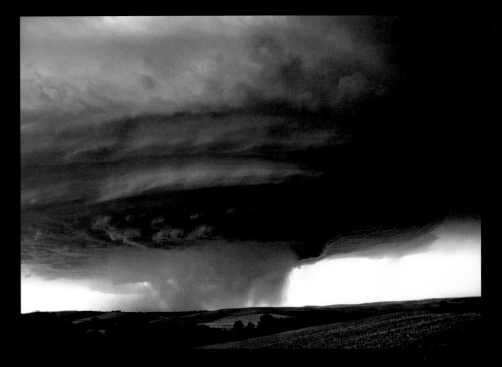

We get closer to Sioux City and the supercell just keeps on changing into something more crazy as it forms into this dough-nut shape. **As the sun lowers to below the cell, I get this shot - one of my all time favorites.**

Even closer to Sioux City we hear the warning sirens blaring. **I wonder what the folks there are thinking as they see this thing approaching.** Some guy pulls up to me: "You'd better seek shelter!" I tell him it will be OK and figure out what to do next. I decide to jump ahead of the storm to check out the hail and wind, but as I rush down the I-29 interstate it gets weaker and more linear, and it really doesn't look like it's got anything left in it, so I figure it's not a bad time to call it a day.

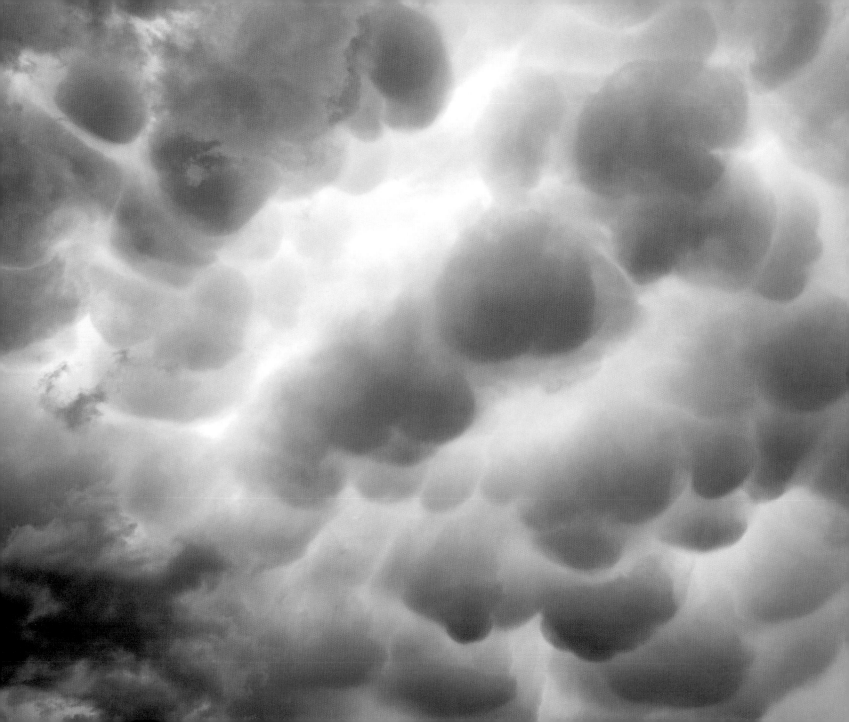

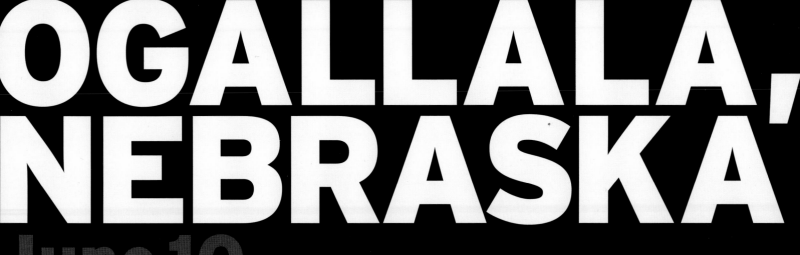

OGALLALA, NEBRASKA,
June 10

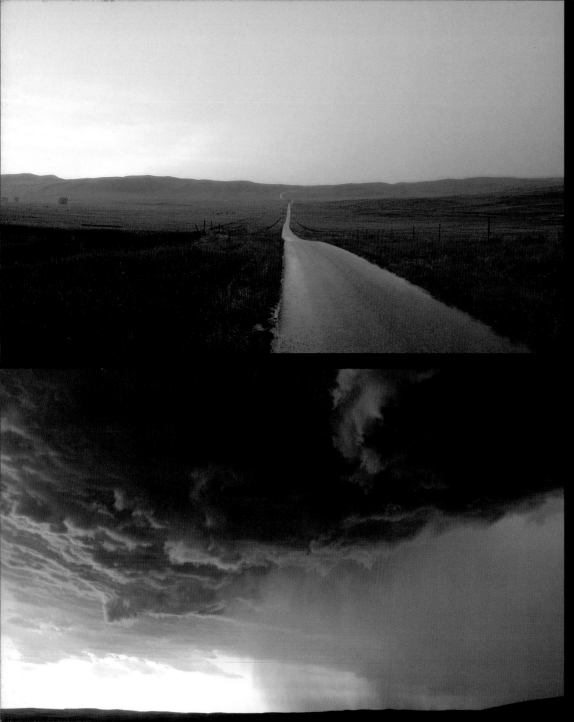

As this storm continues to weaken, we drive east toward new convection near Alliance. We find a single-lane road that cuts through no man's land and it winds us through the hills, right toward the new cell.

On the approach we catch a glimpse of a tornado look-alike outflow finger and a decent updraft.

We sit tight and let the storm hit us.

outflow dominant, so we sit tight and let the storm hit us to see if there's any interesting hail. We measure sustained winds around 45 mph and occasional gusts up to 56 mph and then call it a day not long before Mike starts to chase this gusty storm.

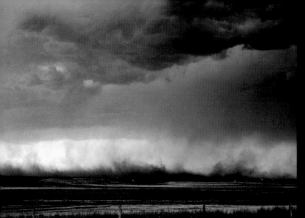

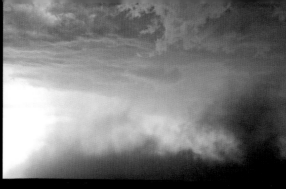

MIKE: The storms coming out of southeast Wyoming weren't that nasty looking, but they had some pretty intense RFD action, which was kicking up a lot of dirt in areas. I love blowing dust, so I was excited.

The low levels out there aren't that moist, so you wind up with strong downbursts. The precipitation evaporates and strong downward-moving air forms – you can see these areas of strong sinking in the patches of clearing around the storm bases. Plumes of dirt rise up and race southward.

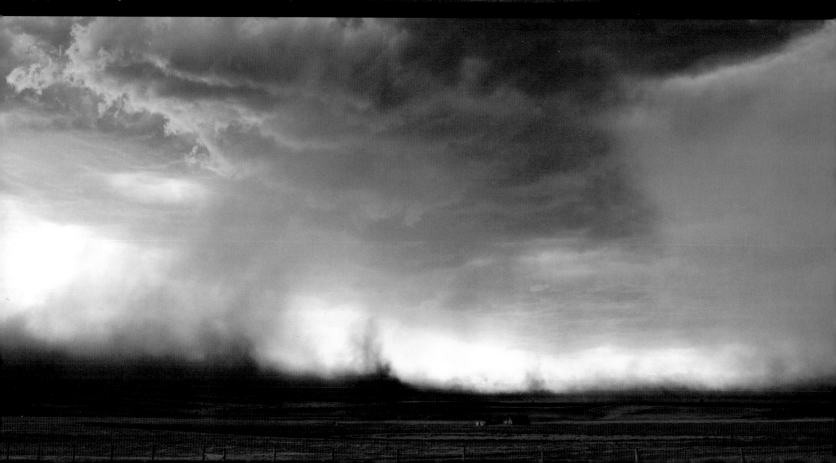

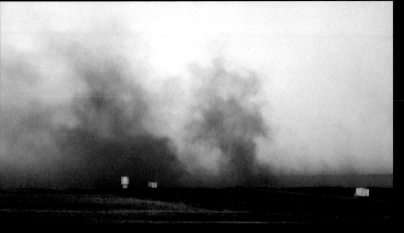
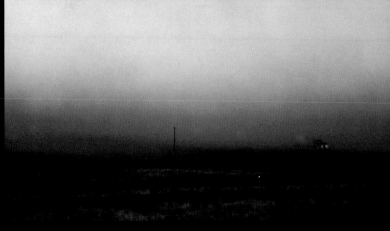
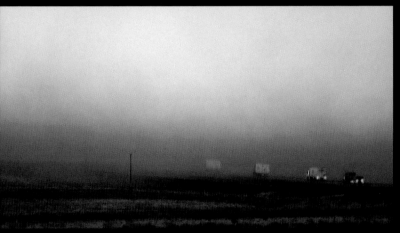
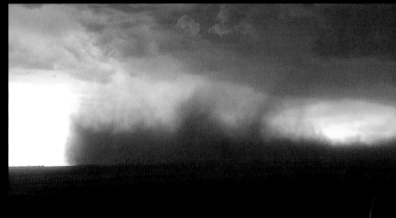

I love blowing dust, so I was excited.

The storm is kicking up more dirt and looking pretty intense around the I-80 interstate. The motions across the interstate are getting real fast and I can't understand why people keep on driving into this, rather than pulling over and waiting for it to pass. You can see here how the trucks just disappear. It turns out that a semi got blown over.

I want to stay and photograph the flying dirt as it gets to me, but it looks like there might be accidents and I don't want to get stuck behind traffic. As it gets a little safer, I fly east down the interstate with the dirt cloud to the side of me. The storm is really hauling now and even travelling at top speed on the highway it's hard to stay on top of it.

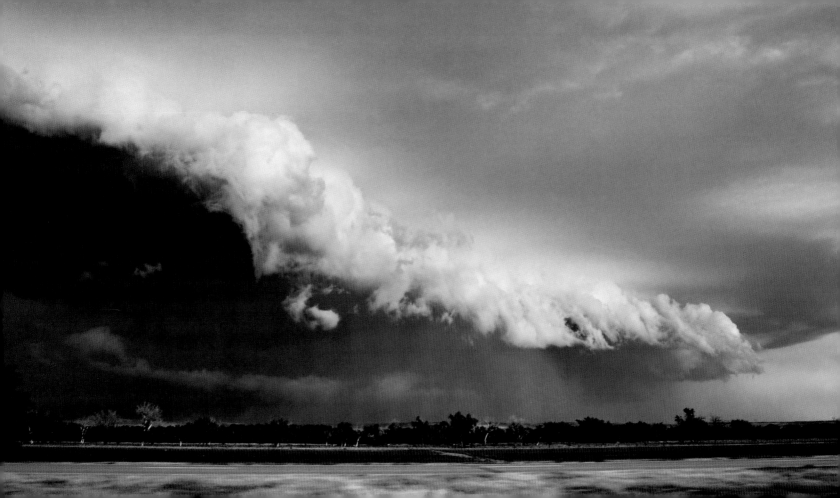

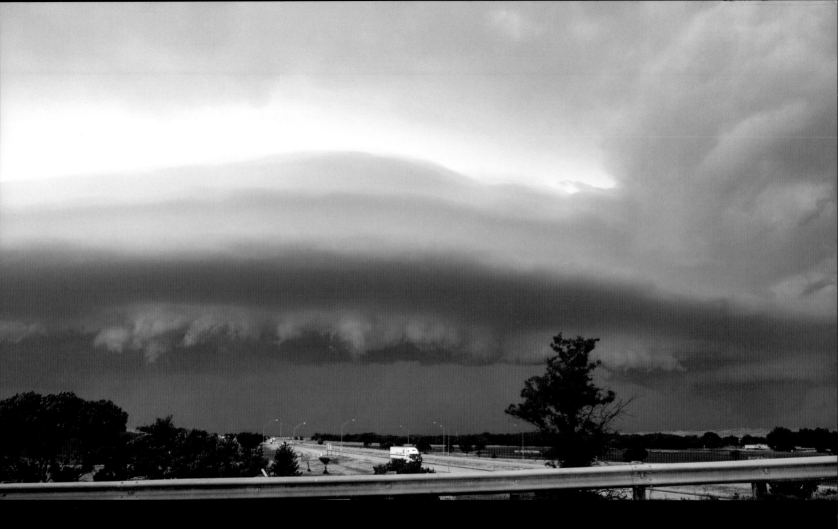

It's damn windy and blasting dirt out ahead of it as it leaps eastward. I'm still racing to catch up.

It's getting more impressive by the minute. I find an exit from the highway and search for a place to catch the structure before it overtakes me again.

Having found a good spot, I'm able to capture the structure properly. It's wonderful to see convection like this right above the shelf. Spring has been tough for chasing on the Plains this year – 2006 was a hard year all 'round, but this isn't too shabby at all.

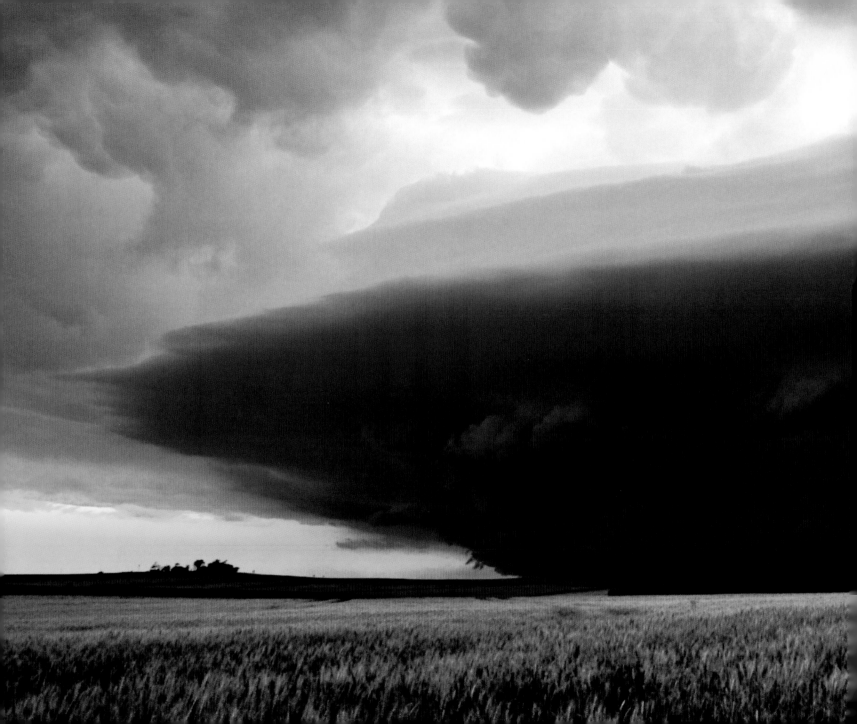

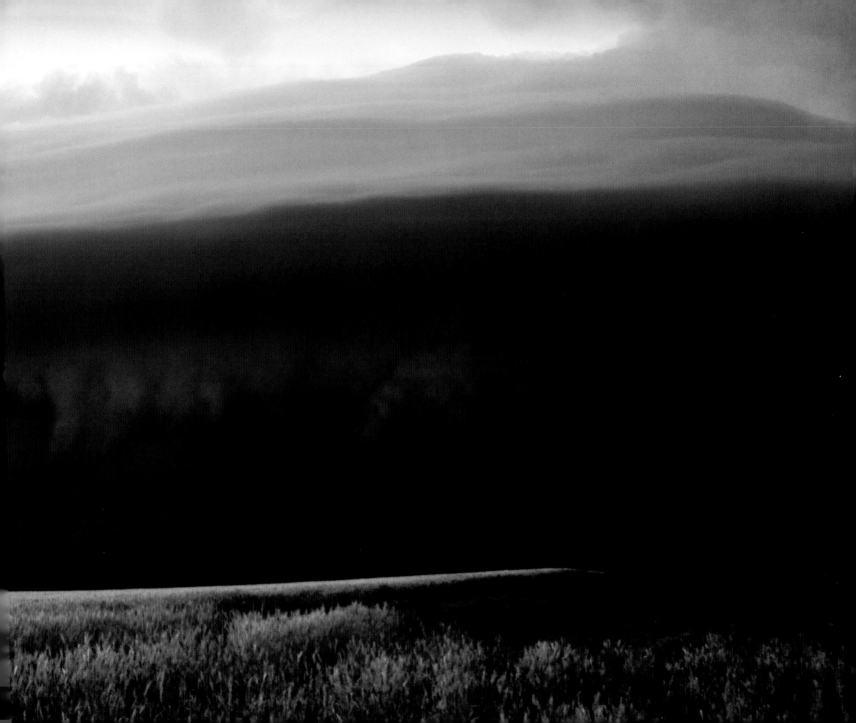

This storm means business.

LENNOX, SOUTH DAKOTA

June 24

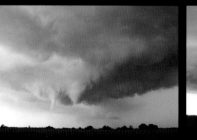
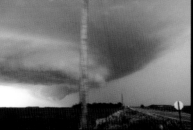

ERIC: An amazing chase of an extremely destructive storm that ripped through South Dakota for eight hours: more that sixty tornadoes – and a lot of damage – were reported across the region. Scott Blair and I caught between 11 and 13 from one cyclic, mega supercell as it zigzagged past Centerville toward the town of Lennox, sprouting multiple new tornado families and funnels over three hours.

We catch a large rotating wall cloud about eight miles south-southwest of Centerville. It becomes very active, with a multiple vortex tornado threatening to reach down to the ground. I can't wait to get into position and set up, so I keep shooting all the way as we blast up the road to find a good vantage point from which to see what this impressive-looking meso has to offer.

A couple of miles northwest of Centerville and multiple funnels take shape, including an anti-cyclonic funnel (the opposite direction of a normal cyclone), embedded in a very violent rotation. This storm means business.

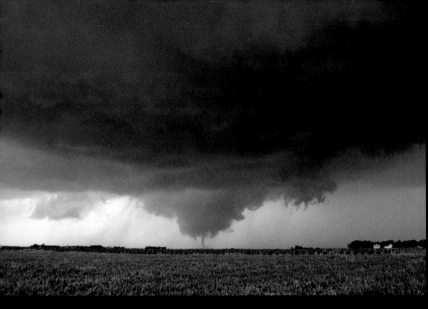

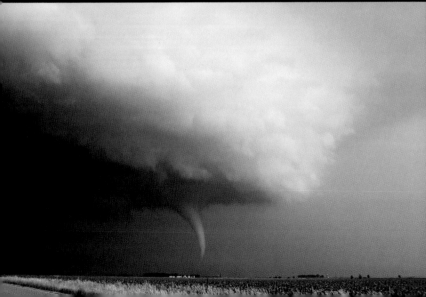

A very significant tornado touches down, lofting a massive debris cloud. You can tell it's doing some damage. Throughout the region, houses were completely swept up and one small town further north was badly hit with several buildings destroyed.

Looking over to the other side of the road, a new mesocyclone develops at the other end of the storm. **When this touches down, we have two tornadoes at once: twins!**

By now it's getting crazy. We keep tracking the storm, as new funnels extend from the cell and soon a fourth tornado reaches all the way down and snakes around on the surface. Normally, a single tornado is a real event, but today we find ourselves saying "hmm...there's another one over there," as if we were counting farms on the landscape.

Normally, a single tornado is a real event, but today we find ourselves saying "hmm… there's another one over there."

One of the satellite vortices must have passed over the road and chewed up power lines. We hit the damage path and people are picking up bits of the wood to clear the road. The power companies pulse those lines with electricity to check what's down, so you've got to be careful around them.

We're held up a few moments helping clear the road, but the storm continues: **a sixth tornado forms with more satellite funnels sprouting around it**, under a larger circulation above. The position gives me a chance to capture some of the structure we couldn't see when we were underneath the vault of the storm.

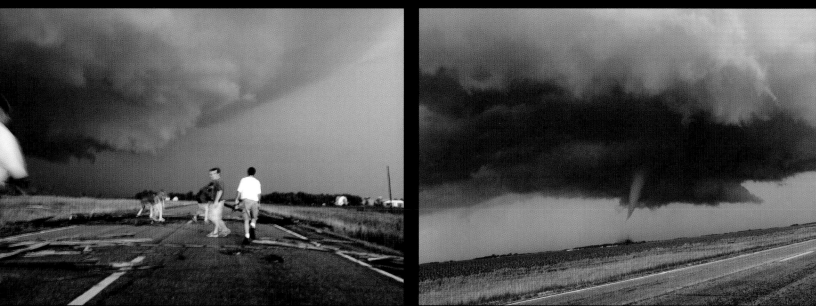

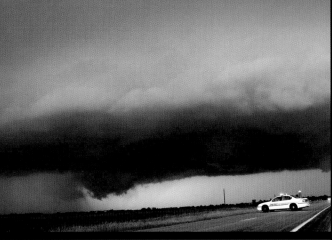

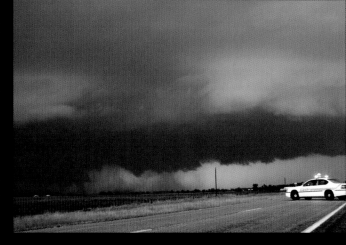

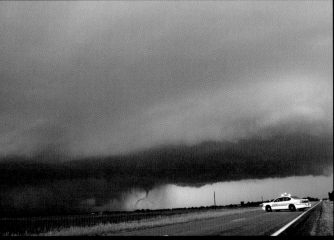

A weaker seventh tornado comes and goes and the storm switches from going west to eastward, zigzagging across the countryside with us in pursuit. A multi-vortex area produces a relatively weak eighth tornado, then suddenly a very strong-looking ninth tornado ropes down (to the right). Tornado eight gathers strength again and gets as big as the ninth. We're about five miles southeast of Lennox and **it looks like it might get hit badly by this pair of powerful tornadoes**.

Our path is blocked by a cop who won't let us pass "unless (you have) red and blue flashing lights." Sometimes they will let you through – after all, chasers are also spotters and we call in tornado reports to the National Weather Service to help them with warnings – but I guess **when storms look dangerous and make them nervous they want to take control**. We choose a long detour around him, get some gas, and catch the storm as the sky darkens.

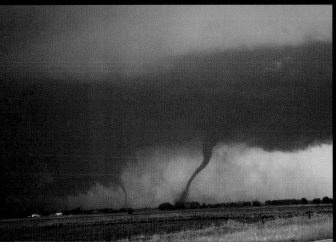

The power is down in Lennox and new tornadoes are causing damage nearby, but they're all wrapped up in rain, so we can't get a good view of them from our position. A large reported tornado is heading for the town we're in and **we don't want to risk entering the highway with a monster supercell bearing down**, plus we're getting eaten by bugs, so we head off to Sioux Falls for some shelter.

The chase is most definitely on....

LIMON, COLORADO
June 2

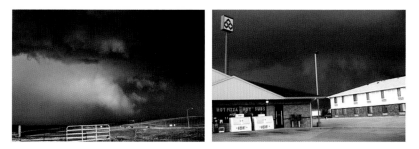

MIKE: Soon after I arrive just northwest of Limon a supercell storm with weak structure begins to change rapidly as the inflow of moist air increases at the ground, kicking up dust beneath it, and aloft, with clouds streaming northwest into the updraft. Gradually a RFD notch appears: the RFD and core start to wrap into the storm pretty hard as a lowering formed beneath the cell. The chase is most definitely on....

There is a huge RFD cut with a serious hail core – this thing is really starting to get going and will soon be going crazy in Limon. Time to dash into Limon, so that I can stay ahead of it and see how things pan out.

I don't want to be messing around with gas later if this storm keeps on building, so I quickly top off the gas tank in Limon while the sound of warning sirens echoes around the city and tumbleweeds race northwest into the storm. **The storm is now raging and is almost overhead.**

MIKE: I speed off southeast to put a little distance between the storm and me, so that I can capture some of the structure. Looking back northeast toward Limon, a long beaver's tail stretches off to the east. As it gets closer, a low wall of scud quickly forms around the circulation, reaching down toward the ground at incredible speed. It kind of looks like – and is at the speed of – condensation forming as you blow on glass, but it's creeping toward me.

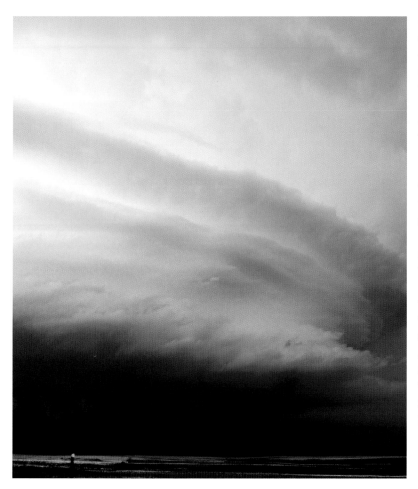

ERIC: I'm with Amos Magliocco and Dave Flick: we've just seen a promising looking storm wash out when we notice a new cell form northwest of us toward Limon. By the time we arrive a violent supercell has matured, with baseball-sized hail being reported along the I-70 interstate. Straightaway there's impressive structure, with a great beaver's tail stretching east.

Weak, brief tornadoes are reported, but this cell is going to be all about structure, so I make sure to stay east and flank it so that I can keep the thing in wide-angle. Seeing structure like this is as exciting as any tornado, and my heart is really pounding as I race away from it to keep it all in shot. Stacked plate structures this pronounced are quite rare.

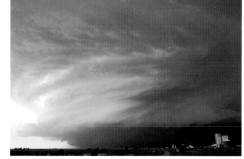

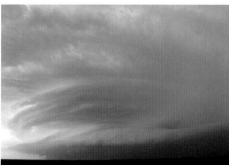

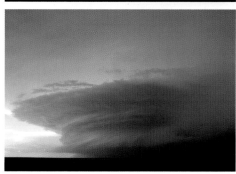

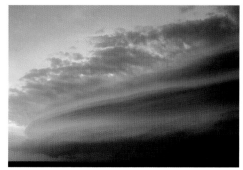

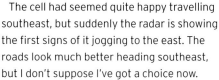

The cell had seemed quite happy travelling southeast, but suddenly the radar is showing the first signs of it jogging to the east. The roads look much better heading southeast, but I don't suppose I've got a choice now.

My heart is really pounding as I race away from it to keep it all in shot.

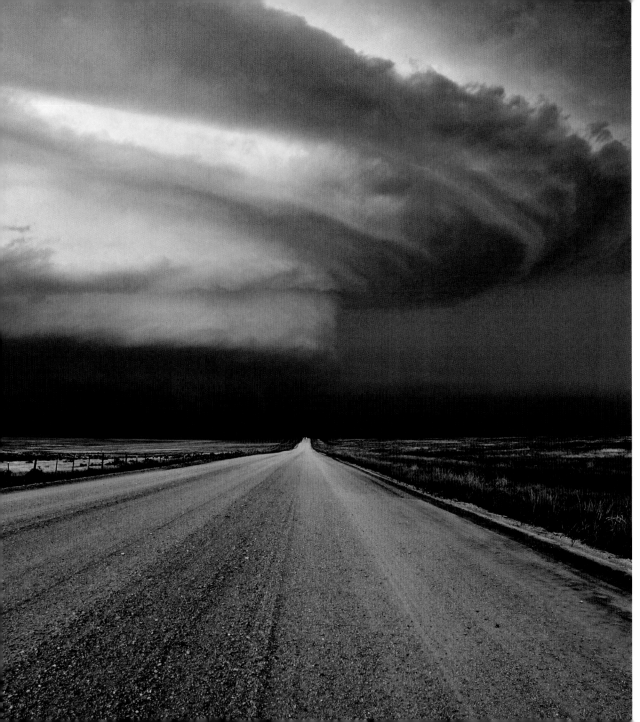

MIKE: The change of direction totally sucks. I have to race along in no man's land on gravel roads for 40 minutes to keep abreast of the cell as it continues to form. Still, it's one heck of a structure and I'm here in one piece, so I don't mind too much. Note the two mid-level bands and single lower band that moved east.

ERIC: We're ecstatic to have caught such an incredible sight, but it starts to weaken and doesn't look like it is going to do much more. We hear about more storms forming to the south, so we decide to head for some good old country cooking in Kit Carson and see what's happening down there.

MIKE: I finally get northeast of it, around Seibert, but it's really starting to lose structure. A little earlier I spoke to Amos Magliocco, who was chasing with Eric and some others, and they had decided to leave the cell and head south. Damn, which way to go now? Normally, if I can't see what's going on with another option and it's any real distance away, and the storm I'm on has any chance of reorganizing, I'll stick with what I'm on already. **This thing is almost on me: it's a tough decision and I really haven't got much time.** I look back south and a nasty looking hail core has engulfed the highway - the decision is made for me. I'll keep going east and hope the storm gods are smiling on me. Or frowning on me - whichever way you look it at!

The two horses at the side of this shed weren't enjoying this storm so much and started to run around like crazy when a couple of bolts of lightning struck nearby.

The storm becomes outflow dominant: I'm pelted with hail about an inch in diameter and it's getting worse. I keep worrying about the horses, who are trying to take shelter by the side of the shed. The storm begins to pull dust from the ground, moving it west into it. **It also starts to get pretty electrified, sending down some pretty close bolts.** I hold out for as long as I can, but need to head east.

The change of direction totally sucks.

I keep racing east, but the cell is losing structure. A new part of the storm tries to get going northeast of Goodland and I figure I can beat it if I hurry: I want to be right in it this time. I get there with time for just one shot before a dirty gustfront sends debris flying and ends picture-taking for the day. **Here, I'm sitting under the storm, outside of a Super 8 motel.**

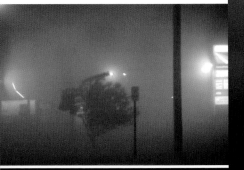

I can beat it if I hurry: I want to be right in it this time.

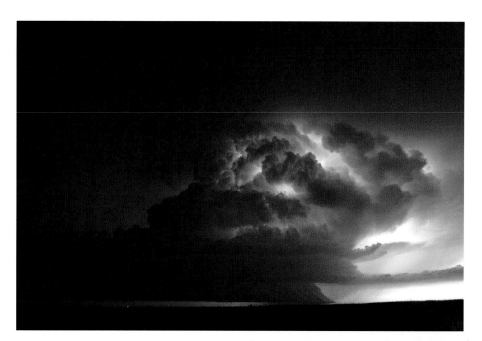

ERIC: While we're eating at the restaurant in Kit Carson the power starts flickering. Our response – a typical chaser's one – is to assume some wind or lightning is messing up the grid, so we check the data out. Sure enough, there's some activity nearby, so we promptly wind the meal up and head off again. We're rewarded with a beautiful low precipitation storm with a barber's pole appearance to the updraft.

Later on that night we stop off again for some convection on the Colorado prairie. Here we are in the middle of no man's land, not a sound to be heard, with the **stars crowning this slightly spooky, silent formation in the distance.**

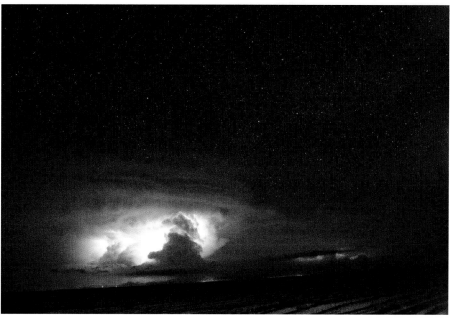

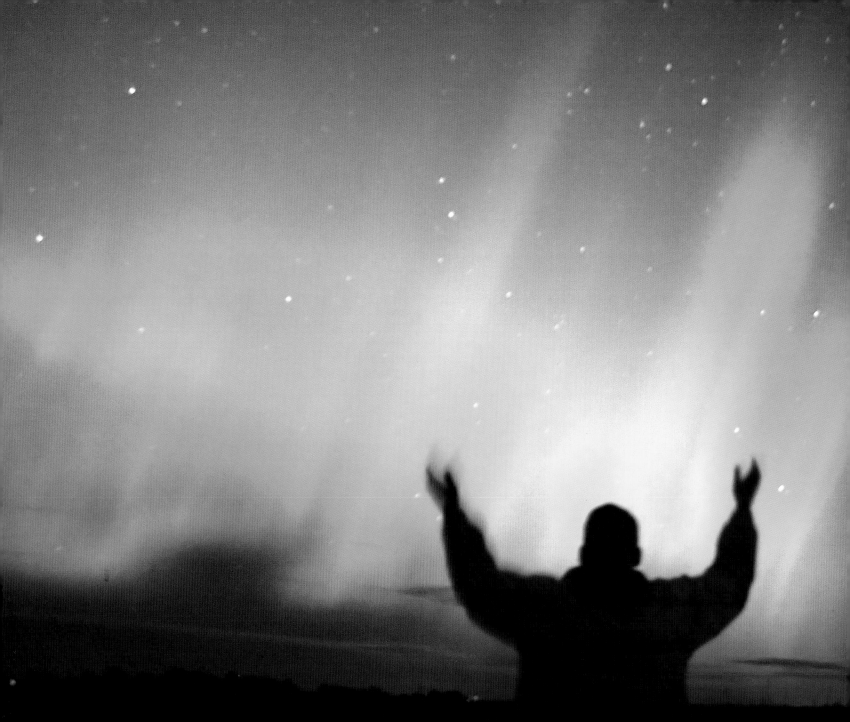

AURORAS

Auroras are areas of lower temperature on the sun that cause sunspots with intense magnetic activity and are more likely to let off a violent explosion in the sun's atmosphere, creating solar flares or "coronal mass ejection" (CME). There is always a stream of solar wind from the sun and our atmosphere repels the electrically charged particles away from us, but some particles get trapped in our atmosphere and are pushed toward one of the poles, which is why you are much more likely to see auroras in the extreme north or south of the planet. The pulses of energy in solar flares increase the chances of these trapped particles and hence the likelihood of seeing auroras, especially further south.

Auroras occur as the charged particles mix with the elements of the atmosphere around 100 km (62 miles) above the earth and give off light. Nitrogen may turn red, blue or violet and oxygen can appear green or red. It is very complicated, though, and there's a great deal that is still to be learnt about the way it all works. When a CME occurs NOAA records it and you know that it's going to hit earth in around 24 to 36 hours.

Capturing crazy events in the sky is what I do, and auroras can produce some of the most stunning scenes you'll ever see, so it's a natural extension of my work. While they aren't storms as such (well, technically they are solar or geomagnetic "storms," but that's largely irrelevant), most people who follow weather events are likely to lean toward an interest in auroras. A lot of chasers won't set out to capture them because the chances of a bust are way higher than with storms and since it's a nighttime activity it's a gamble most people don't want to take, with work the next day. Quite often I've waited around for hours without much indication that anything is going to happen, left around 2 am and it's all happened an hour later. I've never felt like going far to wait for auroras and there hasn't been much need to, so all the auroras here have been viewed from near Blair, Nebraska.

The experience of watching and taking pictures of auroras can be quite different. Sometimes the naked eye can't see an awful lot, but the pictures pick up on amazing colors. When you can see the movement of the Northern Lights (or "aurora borealis") it's eerie and moving.

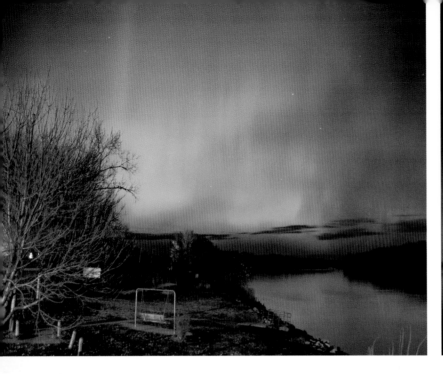

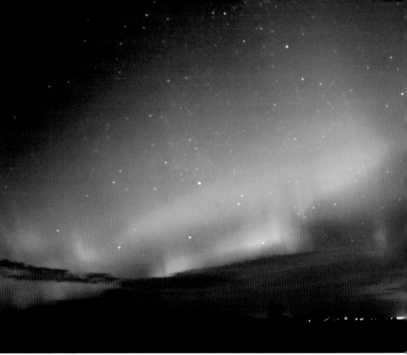

2004 I caught my first aurora in November 2004, and I was real thankful for what I captured. No doubt the situation at the time added to my appreciation of auroras: I'd quit my job in the spring so I had enough money to stay chasing for the season, but cash was running out. However, these shots got picked up on a crazy email chain that linked to my site and around a million people visited my site that month, saving me from a depressing return to "proper" employment.

The lightshow started in the evening with a predominantly green display (above, left), but gradually died off. A few hours later - around midnight - another peak was generating and I went out again. This time it looked very close and not far from the surface, which gave them a more dramatic feel. I ended up settling on a place to view them on the flat to the north of town. By around 1.40 am it really peaked and I was in the middle of a surreal event that stretched across the whole horizon. It was just amazing to see these high-speed vapor flashes going crazy overhead and to the south, looking like curtains of fog moving at 1,000 mph and sweeping around in waves (above, right). Here it comes.... The reds in this wall were very strong and were quite obvious to the eye (opposite).

It was just amazing to see these high-speed vapor flashes going crazy overhead... moving at 1,000 mph and sweeping around in waves. Here it comes....

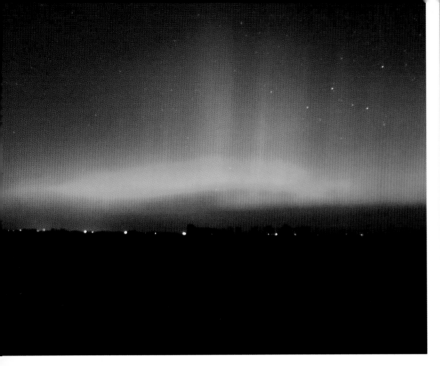

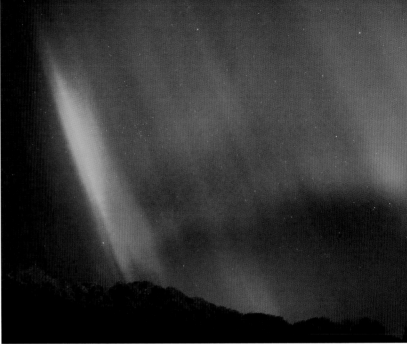

2005 This aurora show in May (above, left) was produced by an extreme class geomagnetic storm, which read G5 – right at the top of the scale. It just went on and on, really getting going at about 2.30 am on a Sunday morning. All were shot with a 17-40L lens, at 400 ISO and most of them at 17 mm at F4 with an exposure of between ten and thirty seconds.

The reds in the aurora (above, right) tend to have less movement than the greens, often appearing as a wall or moving around as pillars of light. I ended up crawling over the roof of my parents' house at 2.30 am to get the best view. The violet colors you can see here are extremely rare (opposite). My dad enjoyed the lightshow with me.

I ended up crawling over the roof of my parents' house at 2.30 am to get the best view.

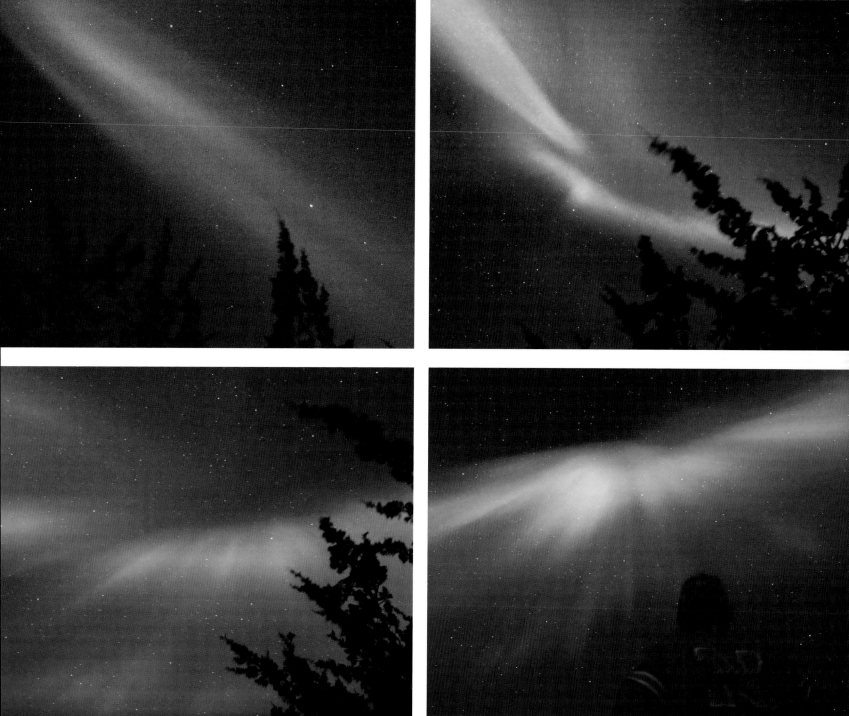

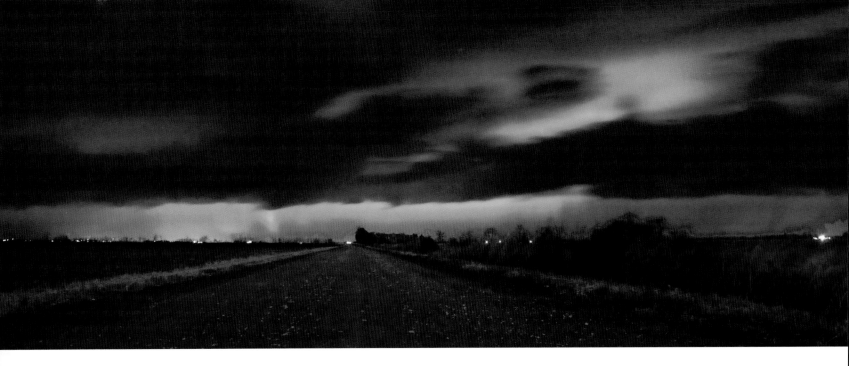

2006 I was sure this was going to be a horrible bust of a shoot. The night before I'd hung around from about 4 am, waiting for something to happen, getting bored, and taking pictures of the car and the sky on very long exposures. I know shooting auroras involves hours of just sitting around, so I'd cleaned my car beforehand especially. I got to bed at about 8 am with plenty of cool pictures of my car, but no auroras.

The CME finally hit the earth just after I had gone to sleep, but it was light so it didn't really show that much. It was looking good when I woke up briefly at 11.30 am, but I didn't think it would last until night. By the time I got up at 1.30 pm a cloud factory had got going and the big question was whether it would stay clear enough to catch anything. As it began to get dark, the clouds gradually dissipated, but you couldn't see much, so I used the camera as an early warning device to spot light in the sky that I couldn't see with my eye. It was a bit of a shock to see them come out on the camera, so I shot out to the north, calling friends to let them know about it.

As it got going it was still dimmer than previous auroras (above), so I shot it at 800 ISO with more shutter. It was early in the geomagnetic storm and the Bz component hadn't yet shifted all that far to the south. Even though it was not as far south as previous shows I've seen, it was just far enough to bring them into view at my latitude. It was amazing to see them showing through the clouds.

As I took this shot (opposite, above, left) an insane meteor slashed across the sky – you can see the start of the trail to the top left of the frame. By now I was with my parents and sister so there were lots of oohs and aahs, even before it finished, while I was just worrying whether I'd caught it on camera. It was the best meteor I'd ever seen and I'm glad to have captured a bit of it (opposite, above, right and opposite, below, right).

Down by the river at around 8 pm the scene was looking good, but the aurora was gradually losing intensity (opposite, below, left).

My parents left, but more friends who'd come to enjoy the spectacle joined me. The meteor activity was amazing and I must have seen about 50 that night.

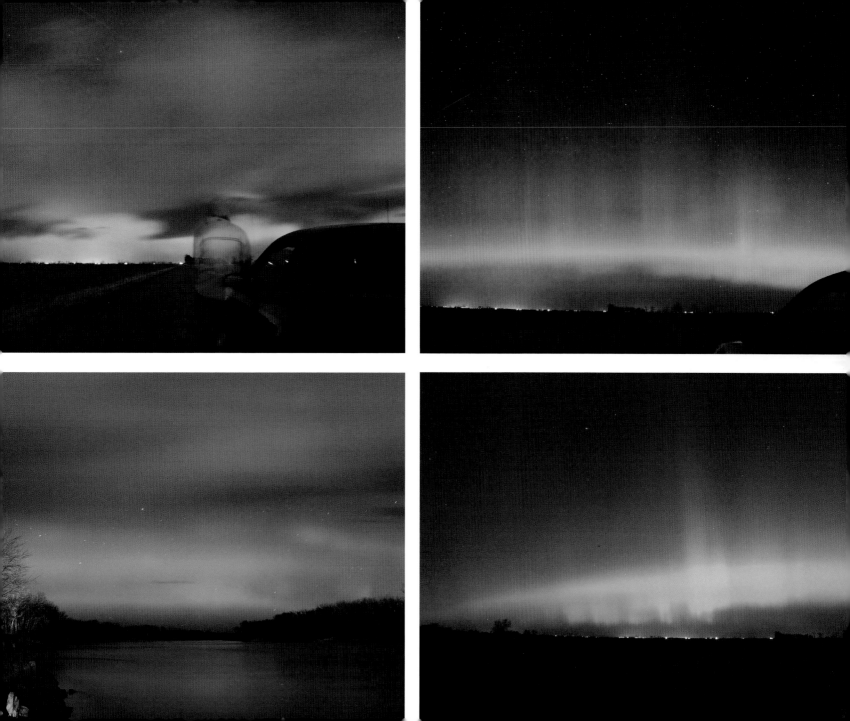

This was one of the most amazing chase days I'd ever had.

GRAND ISLAND, NEBRASKA
May 10

My view of the cumulus overhead had that **"I'm going to bust"** look all over them.

MIKE: This was one of the most amazing chase days I'd ever had. I don't have to have tornadoes to be very happy, and this is a case when incredible structure beat everything else. **Storms like this attack your senses in a big way**: the wind, the shapes, the changes, flashing lightning, and the noise all add up to an incredible experience. It was also nice to be chasing with so many friends.

For some reason my car didn't like me on this day. After getting set up in the car I step out and hit the back of my head on the frame. No biggie, it wasn't too hard. I go back in to move stuff around, and what do you know, I do exactly the same thing again, except this time I almost knock myself out. I'm confused for a little while and have to walk it off before carrying on. The car wasn't finished with me yet though.

I head out targeting a pitstop at Columbus and get data from a motel stop with WiFi. Two areas look good on the satellite - one southwest, near Grand Island, and the other just to my southeast. My view of the cumulus overhead had that "I'm going to bust" look all over them and they didn't get any better over the next hour, so I move to meet up with another chaser, Randy Chamberlain, south of Columbus. This is where the car struck again. This time the door blows shut on my leg, hitting a nerve, and sending a shock all down my leg. Argh! I couldn't feel anything over the tops of my toes, and again I have to walk off pain.

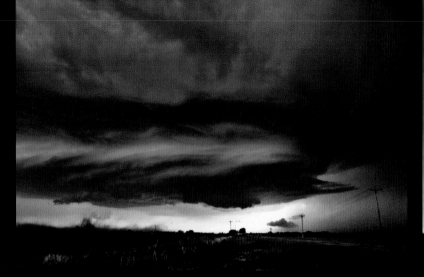

A tornado watch is issued and we meet up with Steve Peterson and J. B. Dixon. I'm amazed to see the cumulus begin to tower because for the last few hours I have been expecting it to bust. Things look good toward Grand Island so we head down there. On the way we hear a tornado warning on the Grand Island storm, but we're only half way there and have a long way to go. **I plot a course toward Chapman with Steve on the cell phone, knowing there is a busy train track in our path, but I hope for the best.** Of course, as we get close enough we can see a train hauling southeast alongside us and we're going to have to step on it to get far enough in front to not get blocked by it at the crossing in Chapman. I guess it was going about 55 mph, but we're gaining on it and it looks like we can make it. **Suddenly a semi pulls out in front of us and we're slowed to a crawl as the train gains on us. Damn!**

For some reason, **the semi driver changes his mind and lets us around**, so I step on it and yank around the corner as the crossing arms start to flash. Three of us make it before the barrier comes down, although J. B., at the back, almost has it come down on him, but he just scrapes through. **Phew! It was a cool little journey by itself, and the storm was shaping up well too.**

You can see the RFD kicking up dirt. It keeps on surging, letting up, and then repeating and the inflow winds ahead of it increase. **A nice beaver's tail starts to form.**

Chasers flee the RFD dust that was trying to munch us for most of the night.

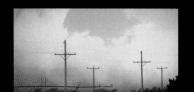

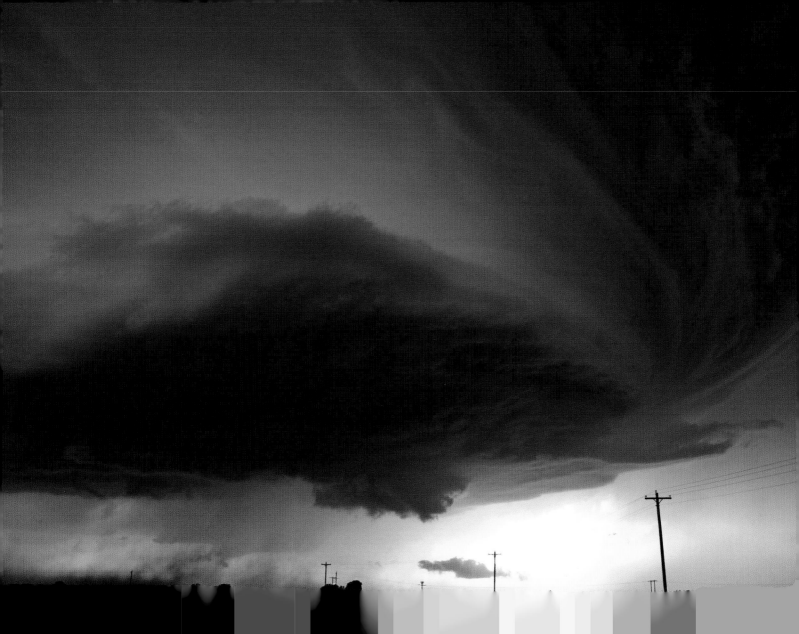

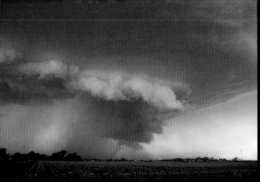
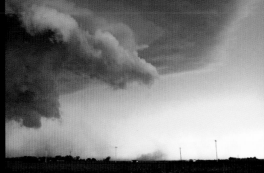
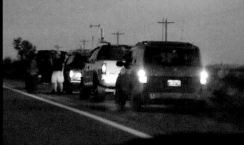
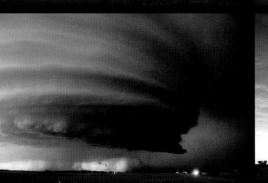
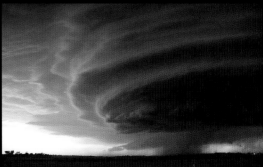

This is really starting to pull inflow now. There are 40+ mph winds with a lot of dirt in the air and this hazy humidity along the boundary.

I guess this is when the picture-taking got kind of fun. The lower the lighting gets, the easier it becomes to balance it, but getting the tripod to stand still in those winds and the longer exposure becomes the real challenge. The slightly longer exposure opens this scene up so the picture looks a bit brighter than it was while I was there.

The lighting is about right. It is getting darker and the sun is probably just below the horizon now.

But getting the tripod to stand still in those winds and the longer exposure becomes the

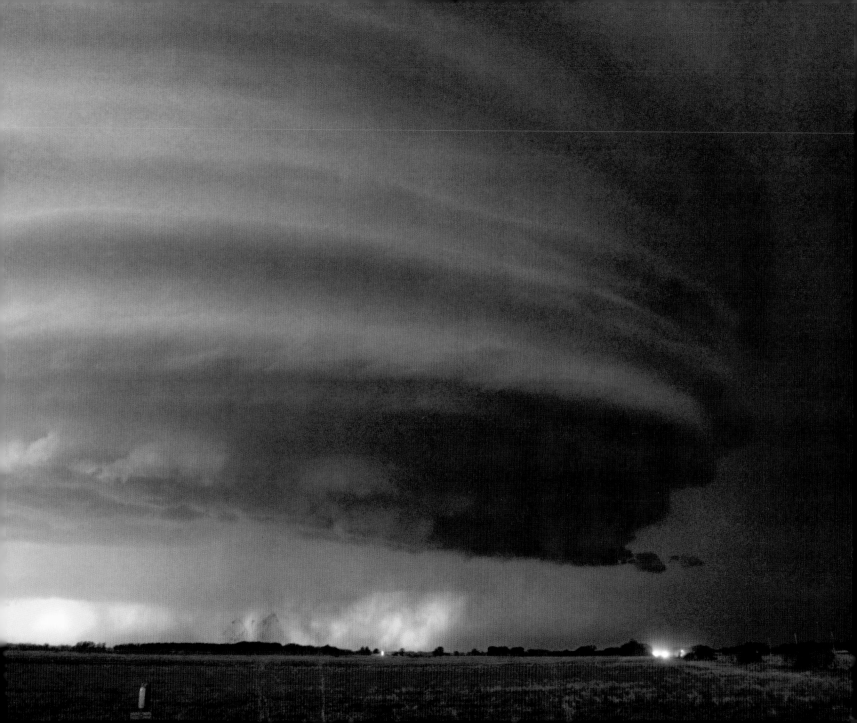

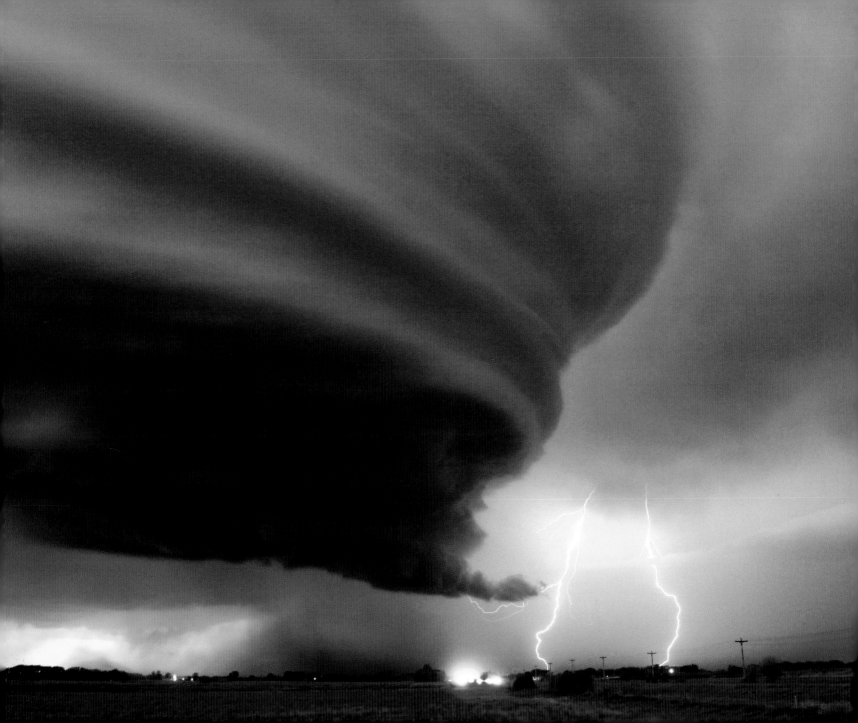

A few flashes really light up the surroundings which make this shot as bright as it is at only a five-second exposure in the dark at F/4.0, but with the ISO bumped up to 400.

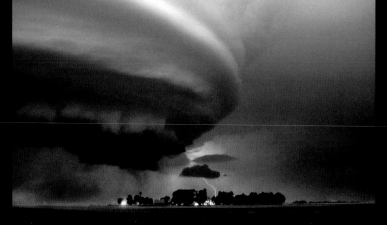

Even though the sun went down about 30 minutes before, there is just enough light to brighten up the horizon under the long shutter time. The streak of light is car headlights.

The exposure isn't long on this shot at all, and it's a good representation of what the structure really looked like. **Suddenly...crack! Another powerful CG shoots from the base. What an amazing storm!**

Looks like the sun is just setting here, but in reality it's already down quite a bit and it's basically night now. I use a longer shutter to catch the lightning and to show the storm structure. The following are mostly shot at 20 seconds at F/7.1, ISO 100.

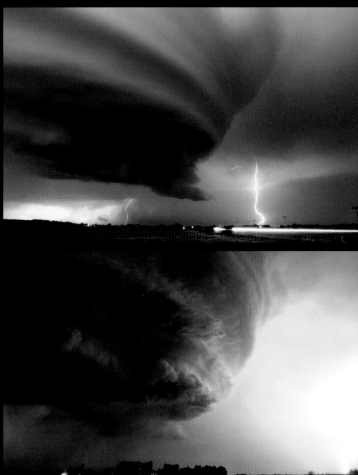

Heading into Omaha to catch the end of a developing bow, with Randy somewhere behind me, **we are blasted by 60+ mph winds that are tearing up trees on the south of the interstate**. Suddenly a branch comes flying from the other side of the road - it must have been in the air for ages and was just coming down. **What a day!**

This magnificent storm has me on the run for most of the day.

HILL CITY, KANSAS
June 9

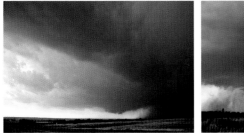 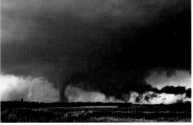

ERIC: Scott Blair and I target Colby City, Kansas, where shear and instability look very favorable for supercells ahead of the surface low and dry punch. An outflow boundary develops from convection in northeast Kansas and moves southwest, just past Hill City. Things don't start too well – early on we get closer to a funnel than I would prefer, but I figure that at least I'll have some cool shots of it. It isn't until a little later that I realize the hard drive hasn't stored the images. Still, we catch two supercells this day, have a real adventure chasing them, and what we see is pretty spectacular.

MIKE: This magnificent storm has me on the run for most of the day. **As much as I enjoy the chase, by the end I'm tired, stressed, and just want to relax in my motel room.**

I'm pelted by large hail as I move east to Hill City, Kansas. A nice wall cloud develops and looks ready to produce tornadoes.

After pitching up about a mile east of Hill City I notice a tornado quickly develop at the base. It becomes very large and strong, with amazing motions as it moves east and then north.

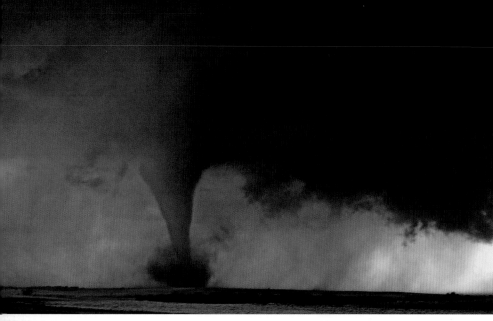

ERIC: I'm already feeling rattled after my close shave, but thankfully the storm has a lot to give and it's still early in the life of this storm. A stovepipe tornado is picking up a lot of dirt and the inflow tail is vigorously ingesting inflow from the north.

The tornado becomes wrapped in rain and loses strength, but it's heading toward us and **one close call is enough for one day, so we retreat a little**.

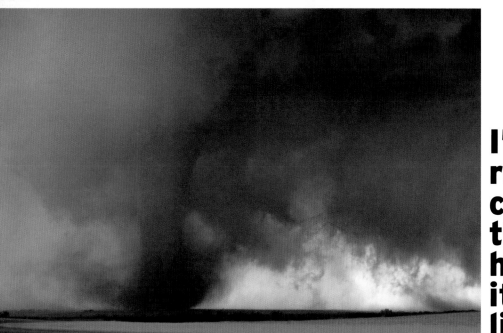

I'm already feeling rattled after my close shave, but thankfully the storm has a lot to give and it's still early in the life of this storm.

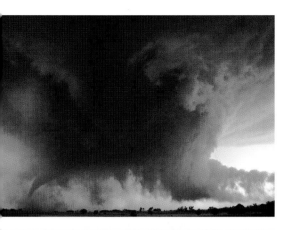

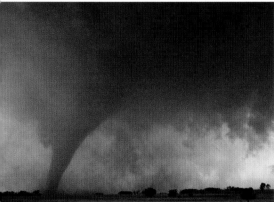

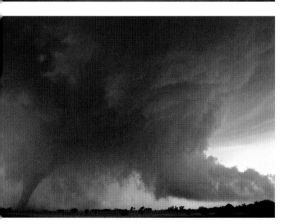

There's incredible rotation at the base – to the right of this image (left) – and I expect it to produce a tornado any minute, but, surprisingly, the original tornado reorganizes, gathers strength to the left, or south, of the storm, and touches down. **The structure is simply amazing!**

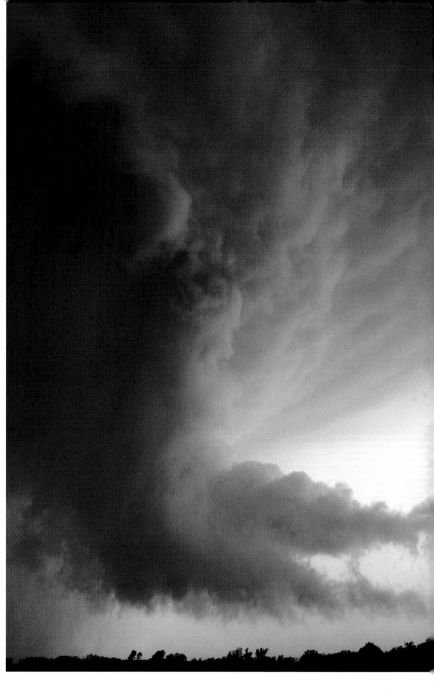

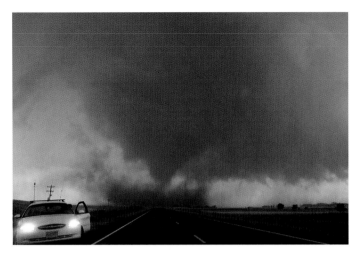
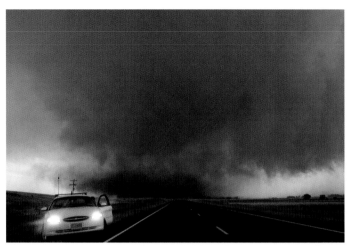
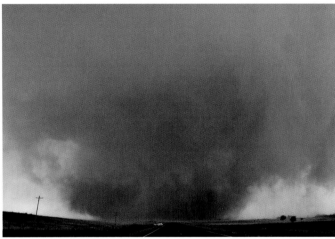
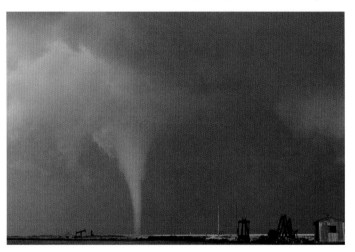

ERIC: As the tornado reaches our road it grows larger and larger without moving to either side. It's coming right for us again - have we done something to offend it? The noise of distant drumming gradually becomes a terrific roar and we're a little spooked to realize it's probably two or three hundred yards away. We quickly head in the opposite direction, worrying that it might continue on this path and wipe out Hill City, which is only a mile away.

The noise of distant drumming gradually becomes a terrific roar and we're a little spooked.

North of Palco, Kansas, we are treated to two new tornadoes that form quickly and touch down. The first is a white elephant-trunk shape with a lot of movement and the second develops into a cone-shaped tornado.

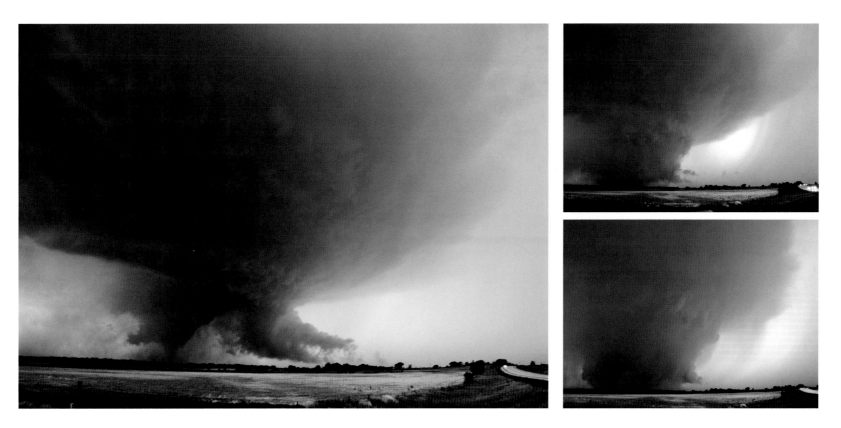

MIKE: The storm now has flat-out stunning structure that coils around the tornado and I'm ecstatic at the sight of it. It's a huge storm and this shot is only the northern half of it, but it's more than enough to be concerned with.

This is one of the worst feelings I've had while chasing: the storm is pushing toward all of us waiting here on the road.... Surely the construction workers can see this thing heading for us?

Condensation falls and the storm loses balance again. Thankfully, it veers south and misses Hill City, but it's heading for me. The hail begins to become a concern as well, so I start to move back. I thought that I had left enough time and room to escape, but I'm immediately faced with single-lane traffic stoppages due to road construction! This is one of the worst feelings I've had while chasing: the storm is pushing toward all of us waiting here on the road, and a huge wall cloud has formed just southwest of us. Surely the construction workers can see this thing heading for us? Their lack of awareness could easily have gotten people killed, given a slight change in the tornado's timing and path.

It's an amazing storm and an exciting chase, but I'm getting really stressed now. There's too much rain to get stills from my angle and my video camera is shorting out due to the dampness. Grrr....

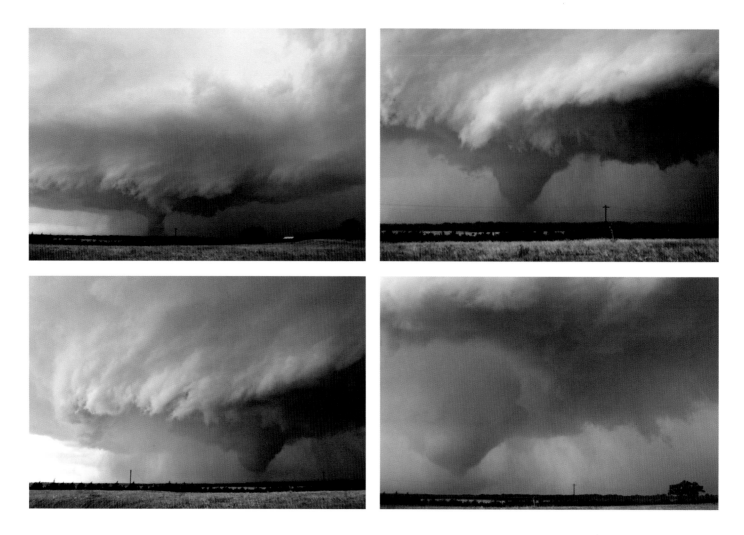

MIKE: Having broken free of the congestion, I get to a position where I can take stills. The 17 mm wide angle makes things look further away than they really are.

This new tornado has very rapid motions and cool structure, but, again, it's getting too close for comfort, so once more I find myself retreating from the storm. A third tornado fires up, heading east rapidly, so I dash into Stockton with the storm on my heels all of the way. An old theater in town has been partially knocked down and it looks like the town was shaken pretty hard. I've spent the last two hours with tornadoes coming right at me and the stress has built to a point where all I really want to do is find a motel room for the night, but somehow I convince myself to go south a little to dodge the storm and check out some new storms that are tornado warned back to the west. **I guess I'm slightly relieved that the storm now sucks and I can get a room at the Super 8 in Hays and relax.**

ODESSA, NEBRASKA
August 10

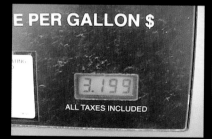

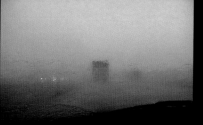

MIKE: I get a sinking feeling when I look at my credit card bills with the line after line of gas station payments. Gas was about $1.20 a gallon when I started chasing, so I didn't really feel it, but these days it's become a real concern. It's staggering how many miles I can clock up on a chase: in 2005 I started keeping a proper log. And it was just over 18,000 miles.

I target some possible activity in southeast Nebraska. I'd checked the gas prices the night before and $2.70 didn't sound too attractive, but I guess I'm itching to chase and I have almost a full tank already, so I top it off and get on the road, hoping that the Blair gas station owners had just gone a little crazy. Three and a half hours later and I stop off in Cozad for gas again. $3.20!

I'm starting to get a bad feeling that today is going to be an expensive waste of time. I end up in a one-lane crawl on the interstate, going right into the core. Good thing this storm sucks, I guess. The whole day nearly ends here. As I get through the core the road clears and I have a chance to get ahead of the storm. I figure I should give it another go, so I pull off the highway. Hmmm...maybe it's not so bad....

I quickly pull over to catch this scene. Be careful with any unpaved shoulders in central to western Nebraska - they aren't called Sandhills for nothing.

OK, there is no chance of a tornado and it isn't even a nice supercell, but at least this brilliant red scene gives me something to show for the four-hour drive down here.

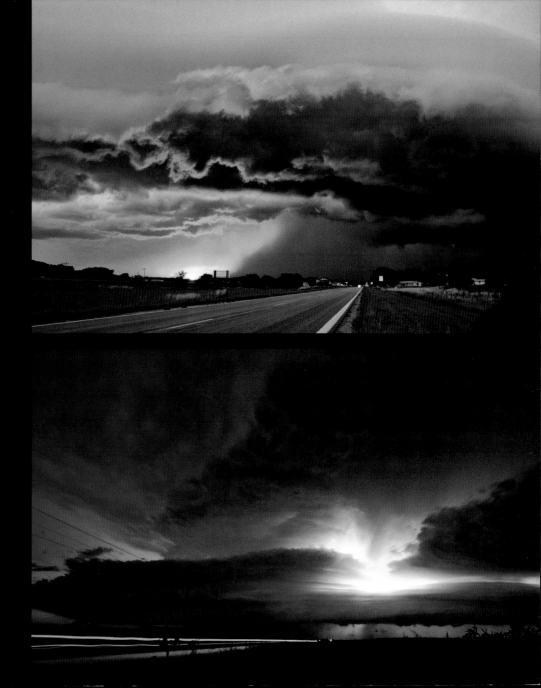

I'm tired and miles from home. You'd think it was time to call it a day – I do, too. But somehow I'm lured down south, turning off the interstate at Odessa, toward Gothenburg, to see if there's anything in a severe storm I've been hearing about. It is tornado warned, but very outflow dominant, so I hold back and watch it move east.

I have to haul to keep up as it races east. It seems to be losing any updraft it had and disorganizes into a shelfy structure with lots of lighting way up in the shelf.

I watch as the shelf goes over me and the moon lights up the front of it. Not a great day – not even a good one – but, **despite there being no great storms, I still caught some pretty awesome sights** and it smoked for an August chase. The four-hour drive back isn't nearly as miserable as I had thought it would be earlier in the day.

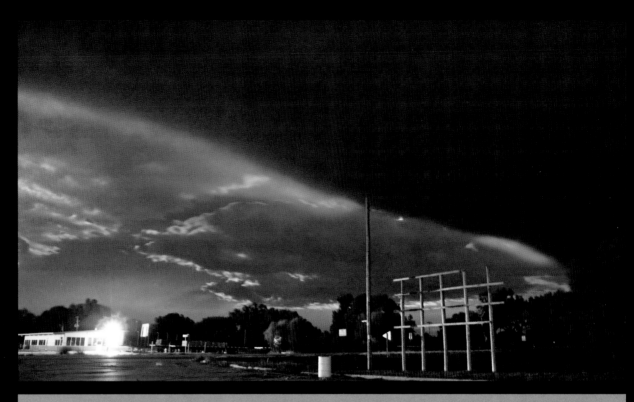

MY TRIPS 2005

March 30 **570 miles**

April 11 **370 miles** / April 18 **408 miles** / April 19 **570 miles** / April 20 **541 miles** / April 21 **450 miles**

May 7 **610 miles** / May 8 **256 miles** / May 10 **327 miles** / May 11 **543 miles** / May 12 **256 miles** / May 17 **600 miles** / May 21 **290 miles** / May 24 **365 miles**

June 2 **1101 miles** / June 4 **535 miles** / June 7 **529 miles** / June 8 **545 miles** / June 9 **486 miles** / June 10 **701 miles** / June 13 **585 miles** / June 20 **680 miles** / June 26 **732 miles** / June 27 **415 miles** / **June 28 520 miles** / June 29 **664 miles**

July 2 **355 miles** / July 22 **690 miles** / July 23 **200 miles**

August 9 **204 miles** / August 17 **701 miles** / August 20 **124 miles**

September 12 **608 miles** / September 18 **360 miles** / September 24 **358 miles**

October 4 **165 miles**

November 12 **325 miles** / November 27-30 **382 miles**

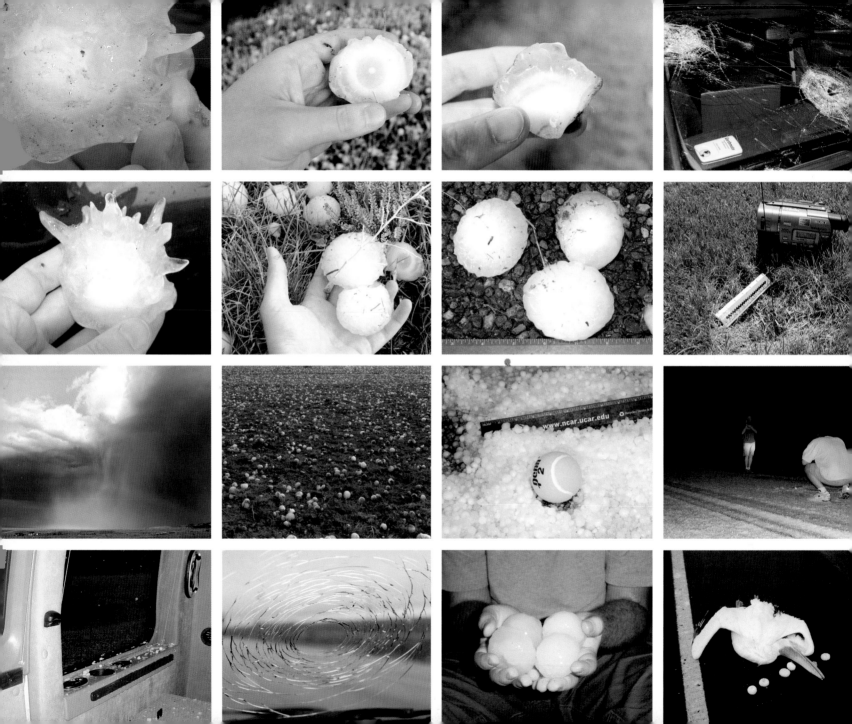

HAIL

Hail results in some of the most fascinating observations while storm chasing. Sometimes cloudy and soft, sometimes clear and rock hard, they come in all sorts of sizes and shapes depending on how they form inside the thunderstorm. Of course, in one sense, the bigger they are, the more impressive, but the unique qualities of the actual stones and the hail shafts are part of the fascination of hail. A scientific explanation of hailstorms is given on page 183.

The largest hailstone on record in the United States fell in Aurora, Nebraska on June 22, 2003 and had a diameter of seven inches (17.75 cm) and weighed 1.67 pounds (750 grammes). Such storms leave the most amazing craters.

Large hail can fall in excess of 100 mph and, as you can imagine, can cause significant damage. Human deaths from hail are very rare, with only four known fatalities in the last hundred years according to the NOAA-NCDC, but the impact on property, agriculture, and livestock can be measured in hundreds of millions of dollars in insurance costs each year.

Many chasers avoid hail shafts, especially when baseball- or softball-sized hail is reported, and approaching a storm from the wrong side can cut short a promising chase very quickly. Large hail can very easily take out all of your windows and on many chase vehicles you'll notice hail dents, chipped paintwork and occasionally fractured windscreens as a result.

Spiked hail is most rare. It occurs when the stone begins to spin as it grows inside the storm and centrifugal force exerts on the water droplets, drawing them outward while they freeze. The effect is similar to water on a tire when driving through an ice storm, where spikes form like icicles on the edge of a roof. It goes without saying that you want to avoid being caught in a storm with these aggressive-looking hailstones.

Hail shafts tend to have a whiter pigment than rain shafts, and you can spot them from some distance. However, you rarely know the sort of size of hail a storm is spitting out until you get close enough to encounter the stones.

Hail can fall in all sorts of densities, but it's not uncommon for it to cover the ground completely, turning a spring day into an icy hazard.

The downward force of falling hail can mean hail can partially bury itself in the ground. The hail may not be huge, but may be large enough to leave mini craters on the surface.

In Seminole, Western Texas on May 5, 2006 we found tennis ball- to baseball-sized hail that completely covered a field after a particularly heavy hailstorm with a slow motion. The sheer density of this hail meant that significant damage to homes in the area was certain, and it smashed the windows of several chase vehicles, including damage to our own windscreen.

April 5, 2003 in Woodson, Texas, was a significant hail day. We were following a tornadic storm when we were caught in a terrific hail shaft with softball-sized hail that smashed our rear windows. It was far too dangerous to leave the vehicle so we had to wait for it to subside. With the roads littered by ice and hail, we couldn't keep up with the storm and ended up watching the town of Graford get battered by huge hail before patching up the damage and soaking up the water. Later, the effects these storms have on wildlife was brought home when we found a pelican that was probably knocked from the sky and died on impact.

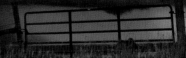

It doesn't take much of a chance to motivate me to head out.

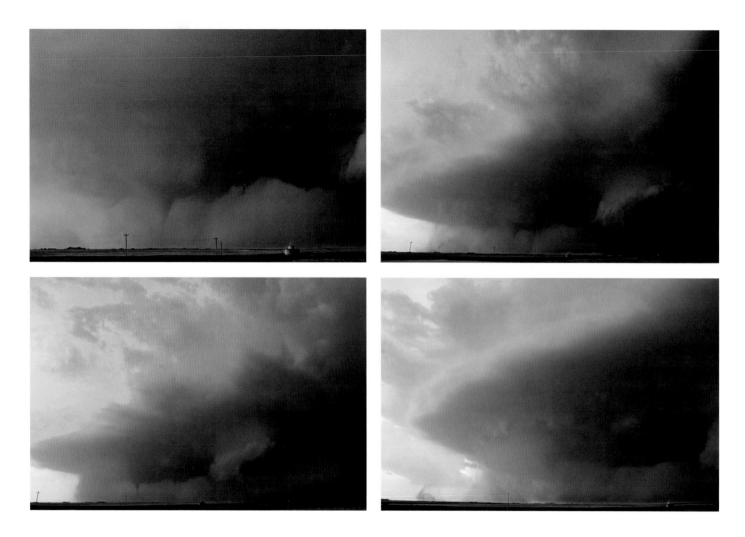

ERIC: At first these new tornadoes look great, but they fade into an obscuring rain shaft, so we decide to head further south, toward a storm that our friend Amos Magliocco was chasing and telling us about over the radio. With hindsight, it might have been best to stay on **our original storm because it continued to grow in strength and show some amazing structure**. The very bad, muddy road south is tricky to navigate, but I'm not disappointed by what we find. The new storm has some stunning structure and produces several great tornadoes.

We were following a tornadic storm when we were caught in a terrific hail shaft with softball-sized hail that smashed our rear windows. It was far too dangerous to leave the vehicle so we had to wait for it to subside.

Wow! A tower was exploding to my south.

HIGHWAY 77, OKLAHOMA

July 2

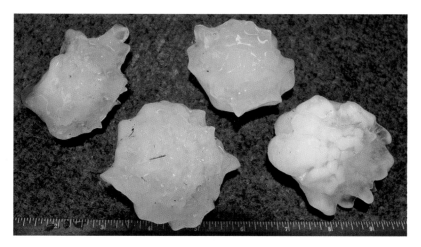

ERIC: July had hit, so I didn't really expected to chase, but conditions looked good for supercell development - high instability in the atmosphere and decent low-level shear along a stationary front - so while I went about my business in the house, I kept a close eye on the radar. I was doing the laundry at around 6 pm when I noticed the weakest blip of rain register, so I took a look outside my back door. Wow! A tower was exploding to my south. I figured it would be worth chasing if there was any precipitation, so I quickly gathered my stuff and went to see what might develop.

Making my way south, just north of Byars, Oklahoma, I come across some baseball-sized hail that had melted some, but it was still 2.25-2.75 inches (5.7-7 cm) in diameter and had retained spiky features.

As I approach Stratford, I can see that the cell is beginning to rotate pretty hard and has an excellent wall cloud. I keep going south to make sure I can get the whole thing in wide angle.

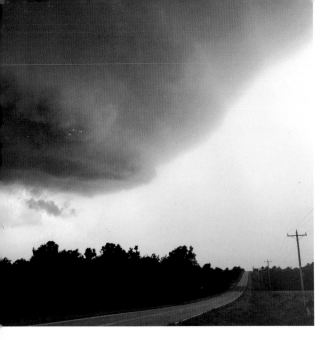

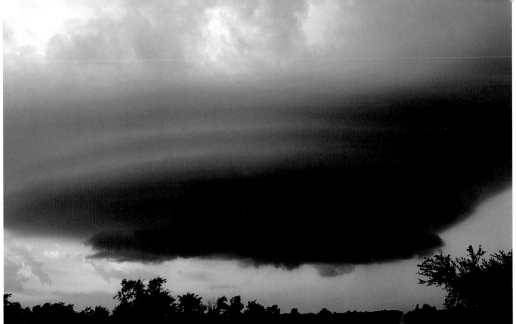

The rotation is still very strong and as scud clouds condense and lift rapidly into the updraft **I wonder if it might produce a tornado**. It has become a stacked-plate meso and is very cool to watch develop from my position on Highway 77.

The structure loses organization and turns into a classic low-precipitation supercell. Perhaps not technically the most amazing cell, but **the setting sun casts a beautiful light onto the weakening structure as it drifts off**. The whole chase had lasted no more than two and a half hours, I've driven just over forty miles and have been rewarded with this gorgeous scene. If only every chase day could be this simple.

If only every chase day could be this simple.

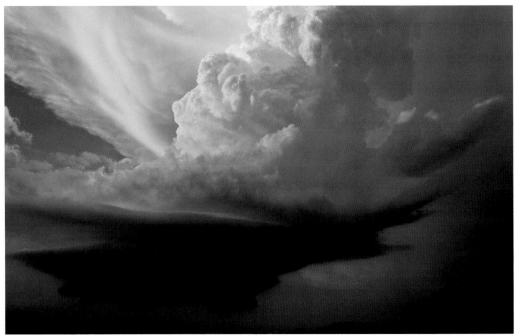

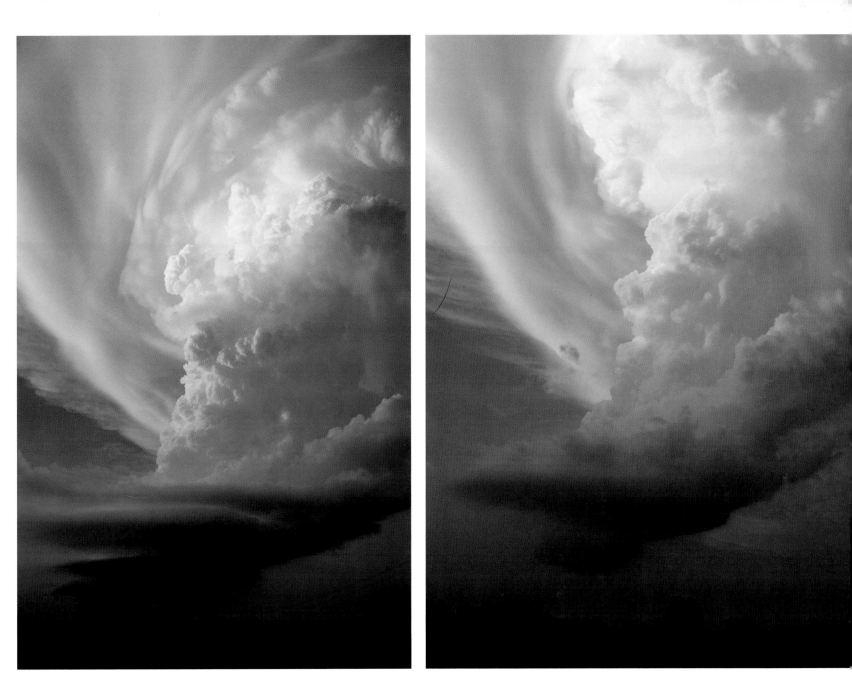

Thankfully, it's pretty weak at this stage, but a shock all the same.

HEBRON, NEBRASKA
May 24

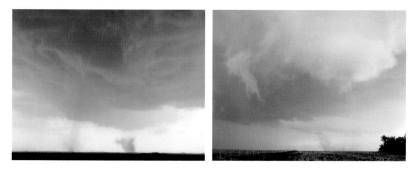

MIKE: I slept in way too late on this chase day. I knew there might be some activity, but for some reason didn't wake until 11.30 am and dashed straight to the computer: already the Storm Prediction Center had issued a PDS box (Particularly Dangerous Situation) at the target area and I should have been on the road already. After a mad scramble to get ready I was on my way south....

   On the way down, just south of Lincoln, I see tornado damage. Driving through two-day old tornado damage in a PDS tornado box...that's 2004 in Nebraska for you.

ERIC: While mesocyclone tornadoes get going to our east, a handful of landspouts form to the west and shoot dirt up into the storm.

MIKE: We're so busy watching landspouts that we don't pay enough attention to what is happening behind and above us: a tornado forms right above our position and we're in the middle of an intense wind with dust swirling all around us, which lasts about twenty seconds. Thankfully, it's pretty weak at this stage, but a shock all the same.

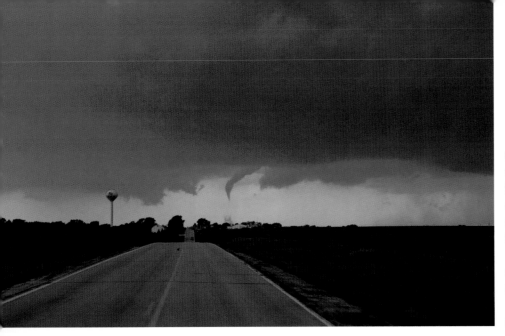

ERIC: Waiting for action 50 miles east of Hebron, we notice a storm fire to our east, but we're hesitant to go after it since the high risk warnings were to our west. **We go east and then west, changing our minds several times.** In the end we settle on west, toward where the dryline and warm front intersect.

Soon after we arrive 20 miles east of Hebron a storm fires and quickly begins to rotate. We race west and catch sight of our first tornado, far in the distance.

The funnel continues to grow into a cone and move slowly east, dragging a brown debris cloud beneath it.

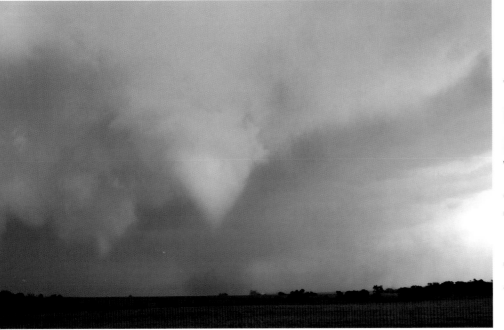

We're so busy watching landspouts that we don't pay enough attention to what is happening behind and above us: a tornado forms right above our position and we're in the middle of an intense wind with dust swirling all around us.

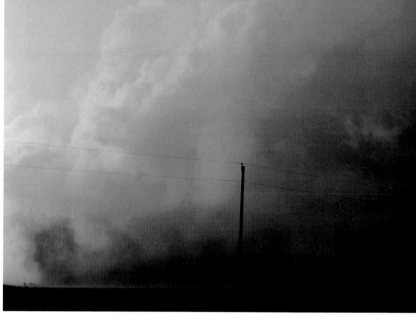

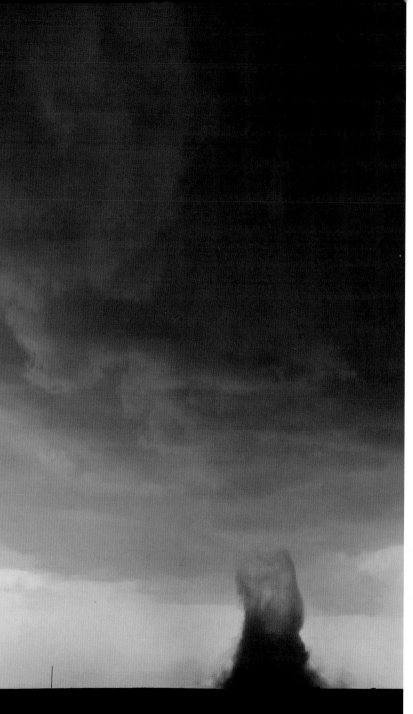

Once again to our west there is more landspout activity, this time closer and more powerful. Dust is over half way up the channel and then begins to fall. It has a very strange motion, like a thin silk dress slipping to the ground - perhaps a strange analogy, but that's what it made me think of. Another tornado develops to our northeast, so **we have three tornadoes touching down at the same time! We're in for an interesting day!**

We attempt to flank the storm, keeping an eye on the cone tornado nearest to us. It begins to rope out and swing south, back toward us. With the winds gusting to 50 mph we opt to sit and wait for it to dissipate before risking another manoeuver.

The rope shifts around erratically in front of us, eventually getting to about 200 yards (180 meters) away. We agree that if it gets any closer we'll flee west to avoid the hail to the east, but it becomes a needle-thin rope and gets ingested by the much larger tornado to the north. We couldn't get a great view of this tornado, but Mike managed to capture it....

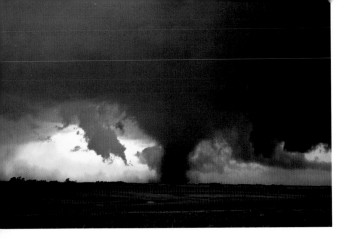

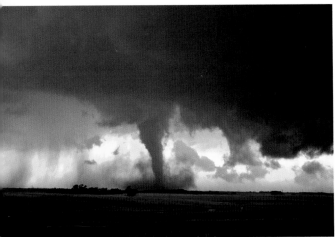

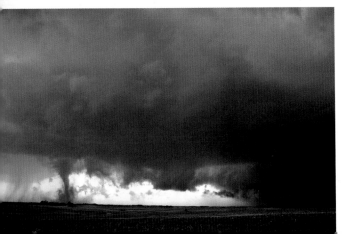

MIKE: This tornado, the most powerful of the storm, starts to plough into the land.

The funnel thins out some, but continues to kick up dust. The debris cloud has a magical motion, drawing dust up and throwing it out higher up, like an ongoing explosion. I wish I had gotten a little closer.

The storm is elongating and becoming undercut. This last tornado is weaker, but close enough to get a nice perspective on it.

This tornado, the most powerful of the storm, starts to plough into the land.

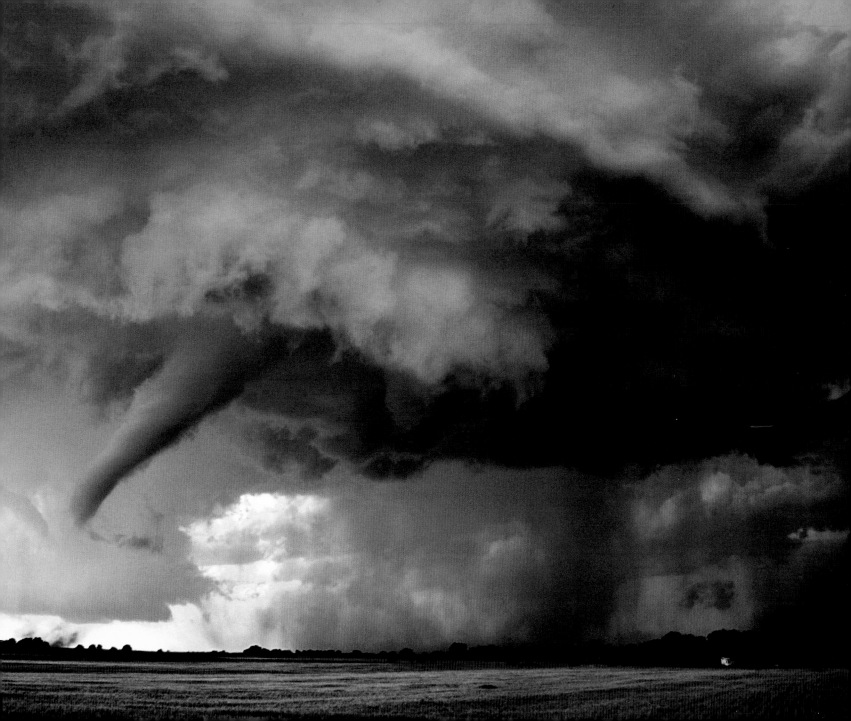

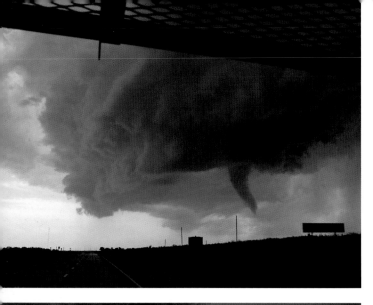

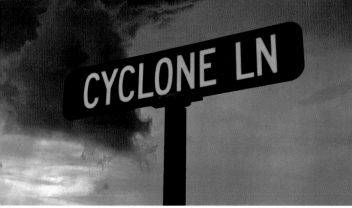

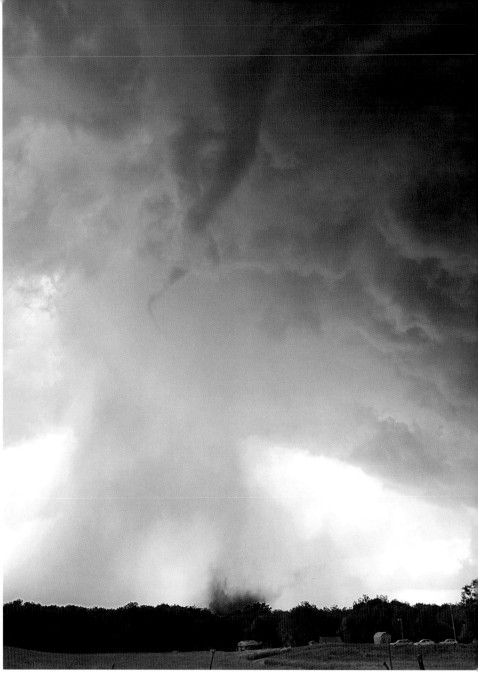

ERIC: Out on Highway 81 in Kansas we catch up with the last tornado from the storm and dash to get up close.

We wait for the debris cloud to get closer, but the tornado dissipates, weakening enough for the winds to push it into different directions and split it into two. Warning sirens bellow in the background as a couple of locals arrive to watch the shrinking tornado with us.

Our chase ends and we pass Cyclone Lane. **One day I'll catch a monster tornado near that sign.**

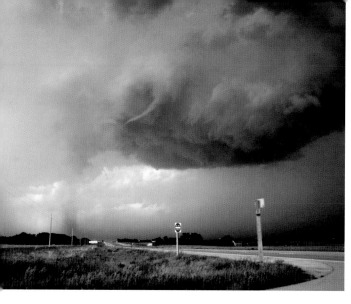

MIKE: The tornado performs a very cool rope-out over the highway. I don't think the people in the traffic even know what's going on above them.

I continue east with the storm as it becomes less organized at the surface, but still has strong structure.

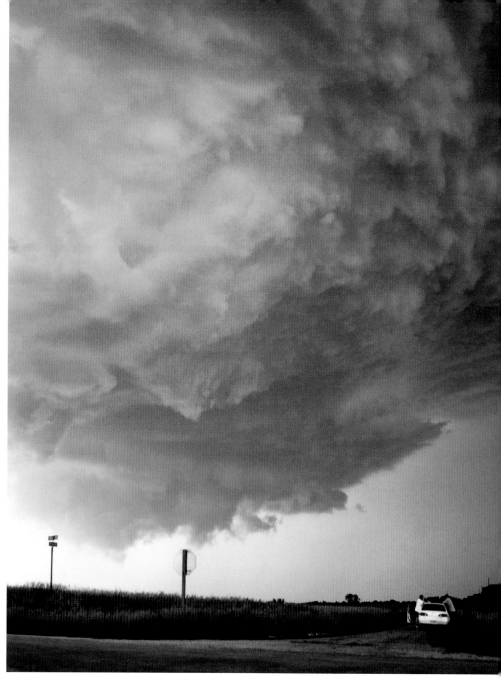

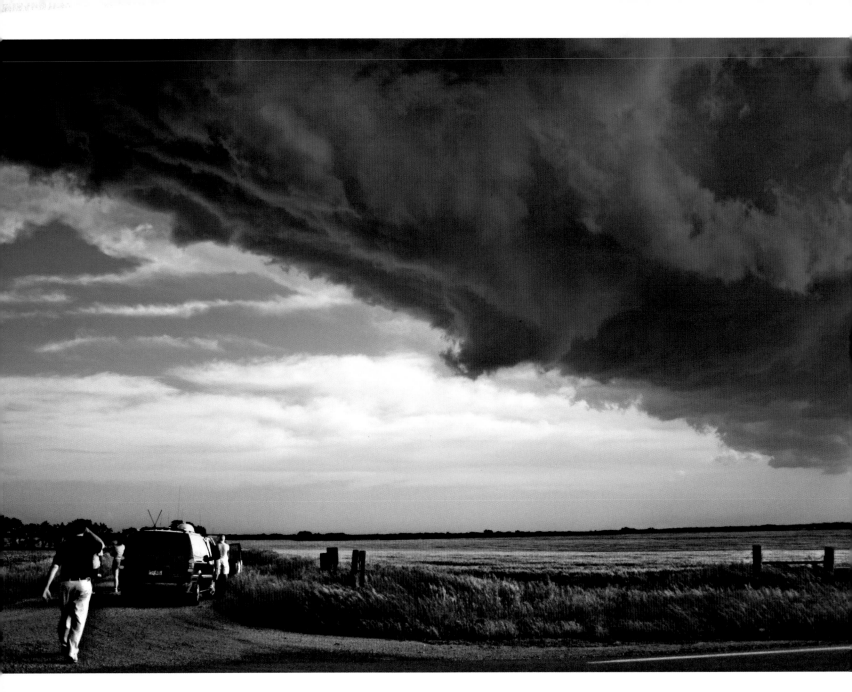

MIKE: I let the gust front move overhead and the sun starts shining under the flanking line. This scene is amazing in its own right. Frequent CGs start coming down and I really don't care to be out in the open with all this lightning, so I hop back into the car. Following the storm east: the structure is still great, but it's struggling at the surface. Time to head back.

On the drive home several supercells go up near Topeka and are immediately tornado warned. **I struggle with the decision about whether to tear after them or not**, but decide just to be happy with the day and enjoy the view of these nuclear bomb-like structures from the road home.

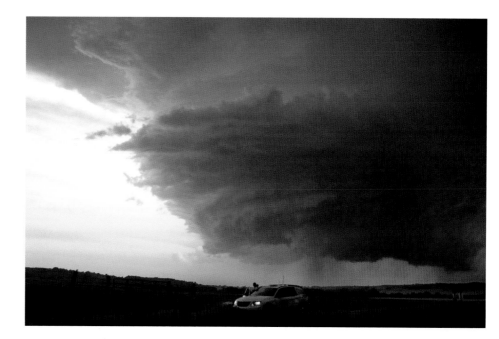

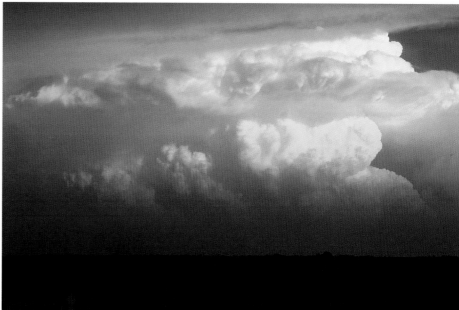

This scene is amazing in its own right.

Sure enough, there was a monster *****ming ***** **les south of me.

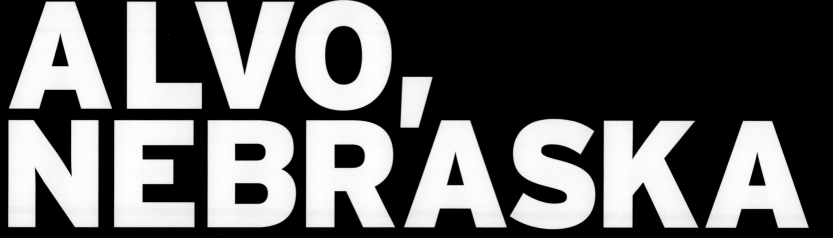

ALVO, NEBRASKA
June13

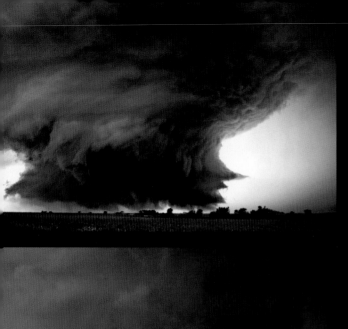

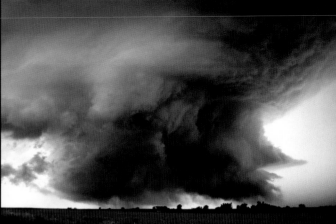

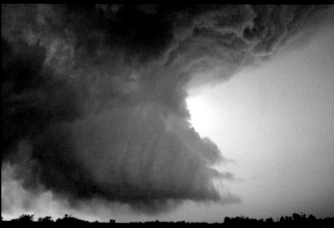

The storm is really rotating and looking crazy. There's a constant roll of thunder, but I don't see any lightning. There are some birds chirping near me, but as the storm gets closer, the chirping becomes weird and stops. Then there's the occasional noise from the birds, but I notice it almost sounds like an "ooooh crap" chirp!

The slot in the middle of the storm splits the lowered area in half. That's the RFD wrapping around, chopping the back portion off. Some strange, small tornadoes follow this process and set off

The evolution of these tornadoes is very strange – **I can't tell if it's one vortex split apart or if it's two that have crossed and wrapped around each other.** The RFD is going in front of the tornadoes and then back around. Rain wraps up the area and the tornadoes disappear. You can still see rotation in the rain bands. I let them almost get on top of me before blasting off to keep up with the storm. I completely underestimate the speed of this thing – I'm going 70 mph east and clouds in the

I'm going 70 mph east and clouds in the RFD are overtaking me.

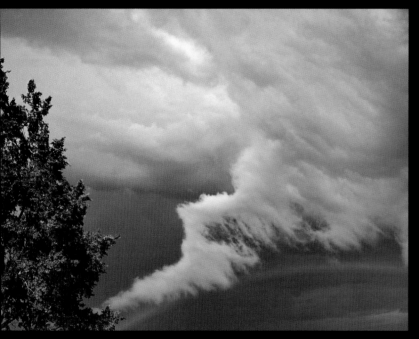

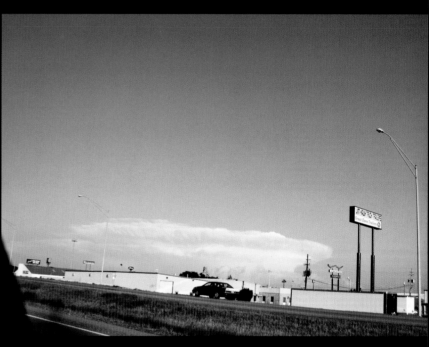

The RFD blasts the cell to pieces. It raced ahead of the cell and left it hanging there with no more surface juice to keep the storm going. Note the scud in the upper left part of the image, ahead of the storm. The storm continues southeast and vanishes to nearly nothing.

It pretty much dissipated, so I speak to some TV stations and agree to bring them footage of the day. Halfway to Omaha I notice a bomb of an updraft going up: this is in line with the storm that just died! **I've never seen anything go from impressive to nothing and then back to impressive in less than an hour**, and already it's tornado warned again. I head off and start thinking I might not make it before dark and the TV station was waiting for the footage. I keep an eye on the second life of this amazing storm from the interstate.

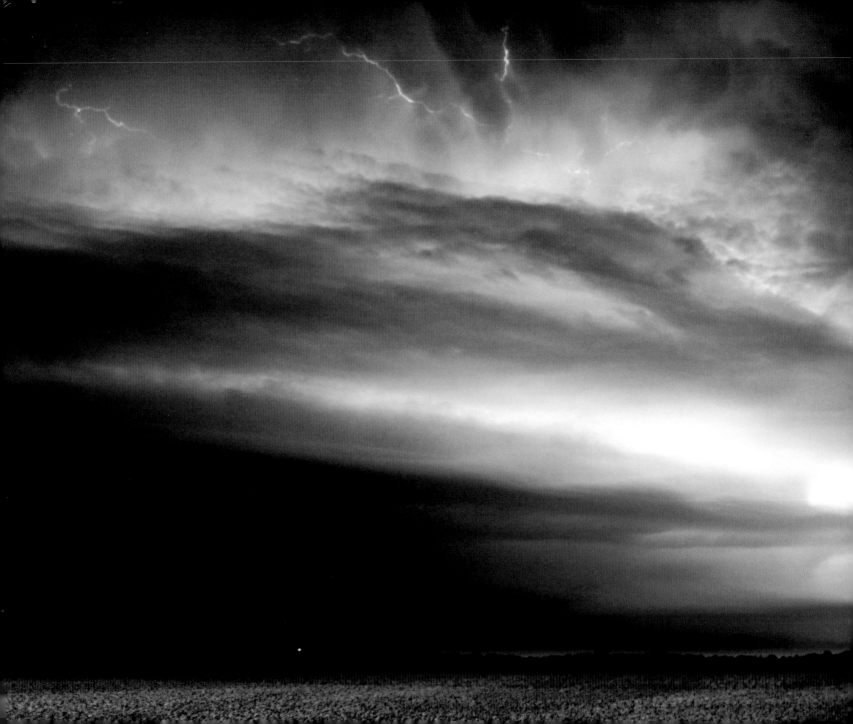

I get back to Blair, Nebraska after seeing the crazy looking storm in Alvo earlier in the evening and **am still up at 4 am when I see this shelfy looking storm**. I guess I'm pretty tired, but I can't argue with two storms in a day. Light from an apartment complex and a really long exposure brighten the field, making this scene look more surreal.

I caught a string of absolute monster supercells.

O'NEILL, NEBRASKA
July 12

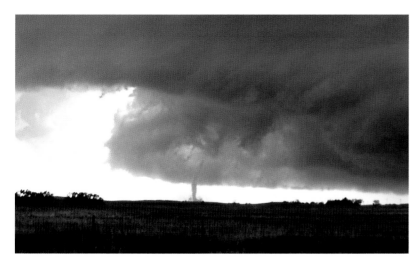

MIKE: Nebraska usually has one of these southward moving supercells in July, but it is hard to know when it might happen and conditions often aren't supportive enough for anything massive. But this day, I caught a string of absolute monster supercells.

I sit here, on the Nebraska–South Dakota border, two miles northwest of Spencer, watching this tornado-warned supercell for a good 30 minutes – **baseball-sized hail is dropping**. At this time there are two major storms in the proximity and I'm keeping an eye on both. South is looking slightly more promising.

There are now three areas of interest, with a split portion off of the O'Neill storm **I beat the core of the split and then the core from the O'Neill storm very nearly munches me up**, but I narrowly avoid being pounded.

I'm driving southeast of O'Neill, not yet knowing what the storm wants to do, since it's only just now forming. Notice how the split is joining the northern storm I've just left.

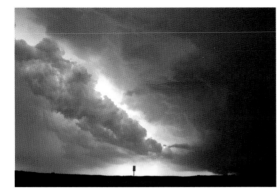

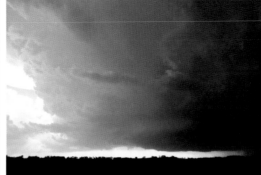

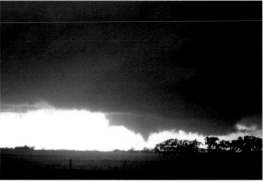

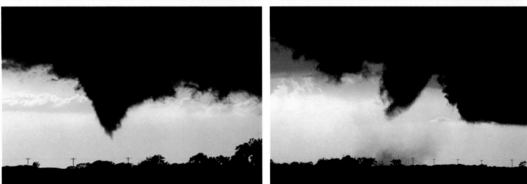

It seems that the O'Neill storm core that I just beat had a nasty core and is dropping baseball-sized hailstones. Looking back at the storm I can see a flat-out bomb of an updraft. The winds aloft aren't supposed to be that strong this far south, but it really doesn't matter when it starts to ride the boundary south-southwest. Convection south of it is concerning me more – I have no idea which way it's going, but I assume southeast along with the other storm.... Wrong!

After an hour of ploughing through the no man's land of the Sandhills on gravel roads, I reach the new updraft south of the big O'Neill storm. The views suck for the whole drive as this convection chokes the northern storm and eats it up. Precipitation cooled air from the north helps to enforce the east-west boundary of the new storm. This is where they merge. Apparently the storm tops are reaching 65,000-70,000 feet (20,000-21,000 meters).

It's barely moving now. I switch to video, all shot from one spot. This is easily the best backlit tornado I've ever seen. **This is the first dust whirl. This thing is huge now!**

I have no idea which way it's going, but I assume southeast along with the other storm.... Wrong!

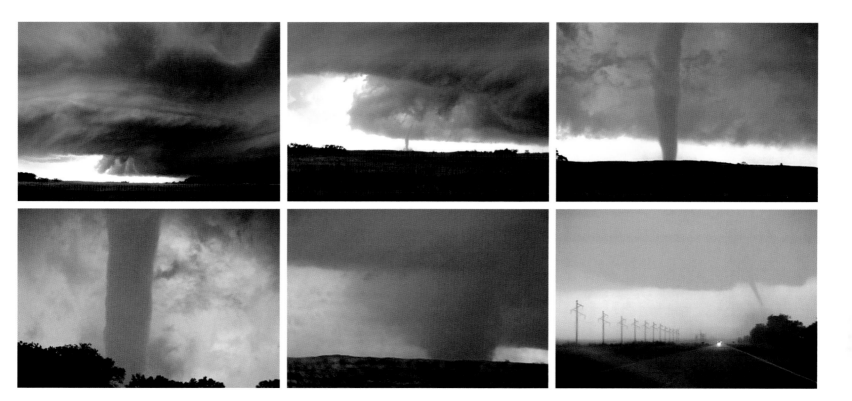

The east-west inflow area is going crazy. Look how rounded the storm is, with the wall of inflow stretching east of it.

A snaky tornado forms rapidly. The tornado was in this state for most of its life. It starts to widen and I finally get some precipitation at my location. It hardly moves at all and stays like this for over five minutes.

The rain kicks in and it turns into this very wide barrel, all wrapped up in rain. **Somewhere in there are two houses that got taken out.**

I position myself in front of the tornado and plan to drop south quickly when I notice a new tornado form to the west.

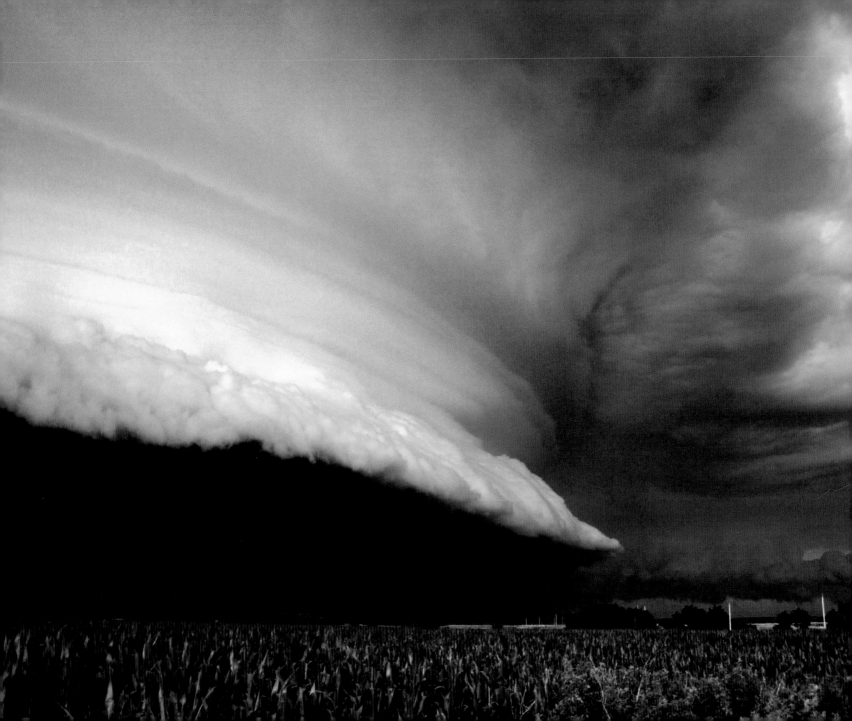

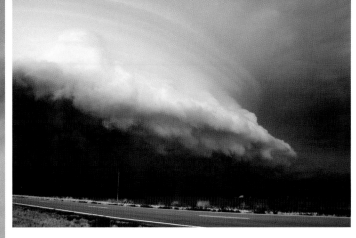

I mess around trying to alter my course as it changes direction, turning from heading south-south westerly to go south and then east. I am doing 70 mph on the highway and it's trying to pass me overhead. I am southeast of North Loup and **what a monster it has become!**

I finally get a chance to pull over and take in the view, looking west...and north. I told you it was a monster. To top it all off, it was covering the entire sky.

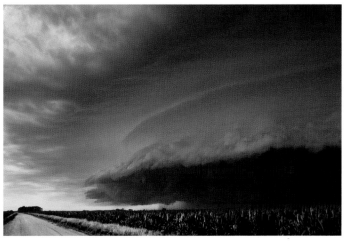

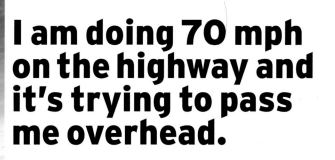

I am doing 70 mph on the highway and it's trying to pass me overhead.

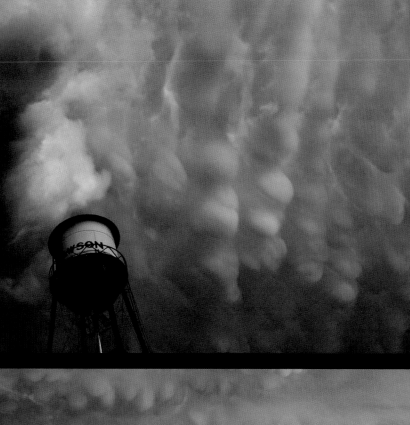

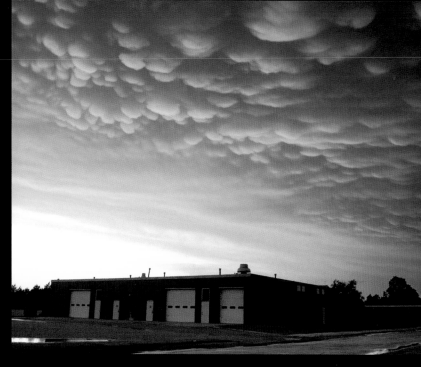

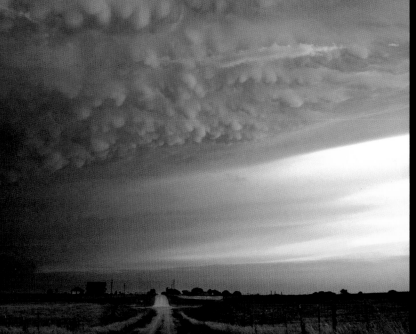

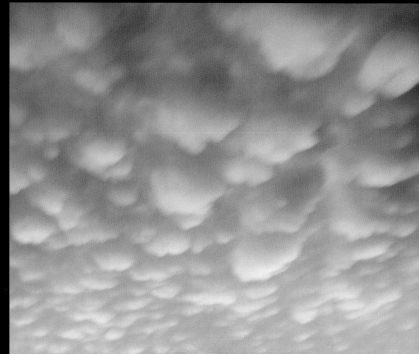

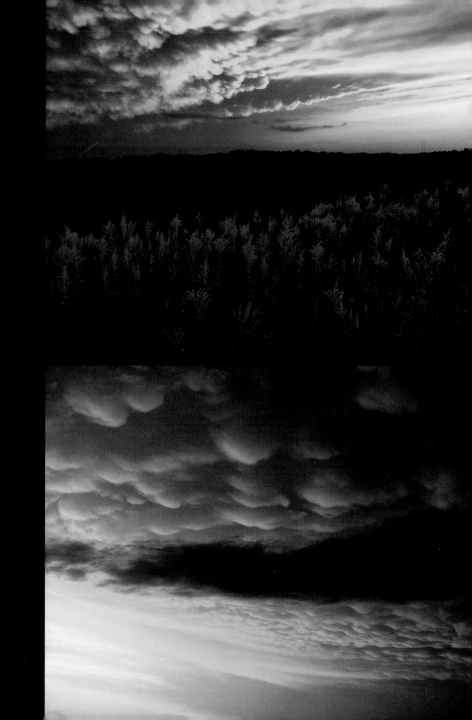

MAMMATUS

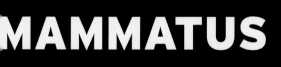

There is a common misconception that mammatus clouds indicate that a tornado is coming or that severe weather will occur. Mammatus clouds typically form under the anvils of thunderstorms, however, they can also occur in almost any cloud type in non-storm environments. These photos show mammatus clouds usually associated with strong to severe thunderstorms, in which they are typically much more pronounced.

The underside of thunderstorm anvils are associated with sharp vertical temperature, moisture, and wind shear gradients, separating moisture anvil cloud from the surrounding dry atmosphere. The anvil cloud consists mainly of ice particles that begin to descend back to earth. It is during this phase that mammatus begin to form, possibly by sublimation of the particles as they fall into round cotton-ball shapes. Scientists still don't know exactly why they form as very few observations have been taken during these events.

Mammatus can last from 15 minutes to over an hour, however, each individual lobe may last only 10 minutes, before they are replaced with new lobes protruding downward from the anvil. Each lobe is from 820 ft (250 meters) to over 3,000 ft (900 meters) to over a kilometer in diameter.

Sunsets add a new element into the beauty of mammatus clouds. As the sun sets, the low angle of the sun begins to reach the underside of thunderstorm anvil, turning the typical grey scene into an illuminated gold or red color, with each lobe causing a shadow on surrounding lobes. It is during this time that mammatus are often at their most beautiful.

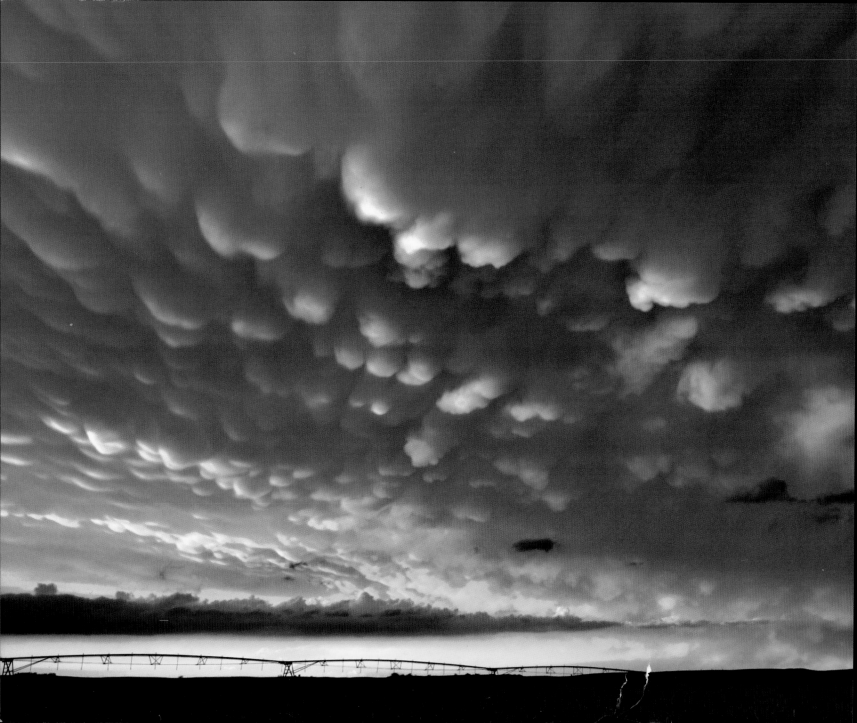

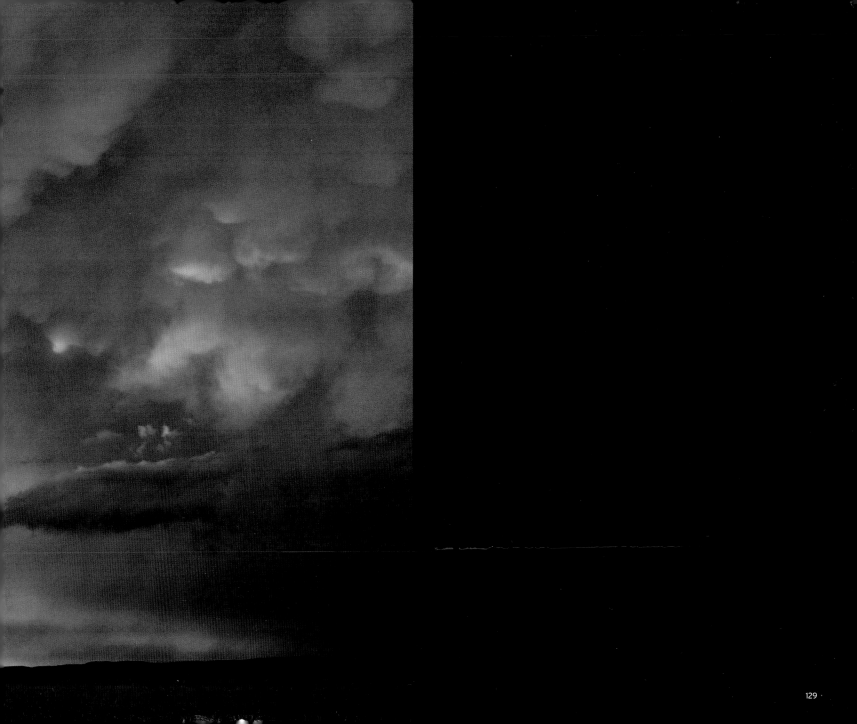

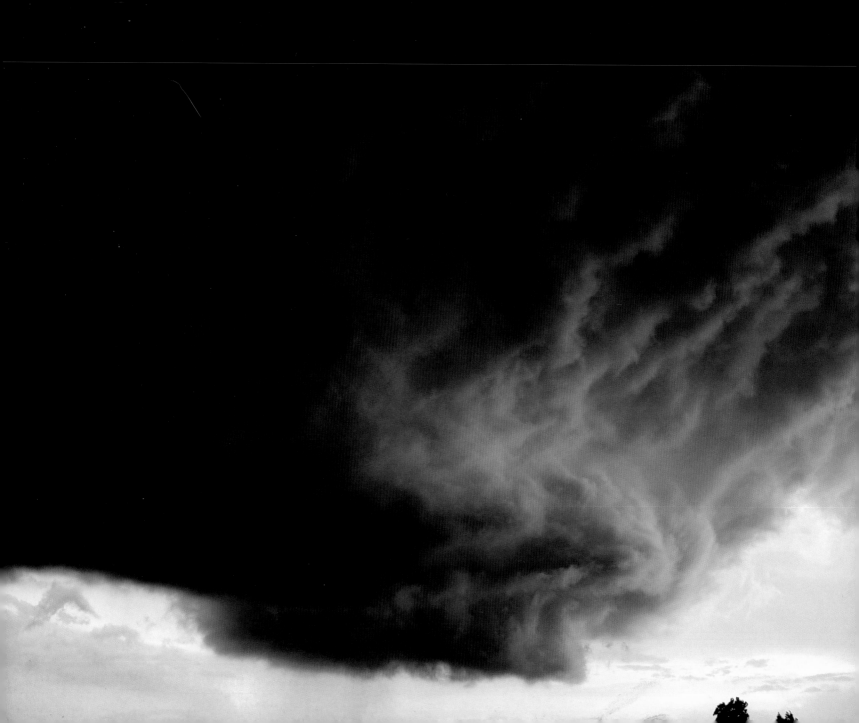

FALLS CITY, NEBRASKA

July 26

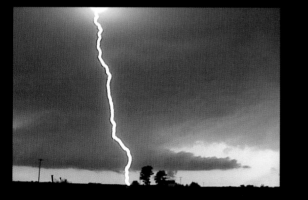

MIKE: My five megapixel Sony dsc-F707 had seemed such a risky investment at the time, but getting a decent stills camera was one of the best moves I've made. Up until this point, I had just been using the video camera to record what I was seeing, but as I got more experience chasing I was seeing more things that really deserved to be captured in a higher resolution. I definitely struck it lucky on this first outing with my new camera, even if I hadn't yet found my feet with shooting stills. Thankfully, digital cameras are pretty darn simple to work out – especially since you can see the results straightaway – so I returned with pictures that quickly made me feel better about spending $1,000 on a camera.

I've been watching elevated cloud garbage way up in the sky for an hour or so. The dew-saturated air suggests something is going to happen with this storm. I notice a persistent block of scud clouds to my southwest and figure it marks the boundary that will kick-start the action, so I head south. The storm isn't going to wait for me and on the way it lets loose with a few massive bolts of lighting that hit the ground (CGs). I've never been so near to this many CGs before. Juggling the stills camera and the video camera is proving tricky and the CGs jolt me into my default video-capturing at first.

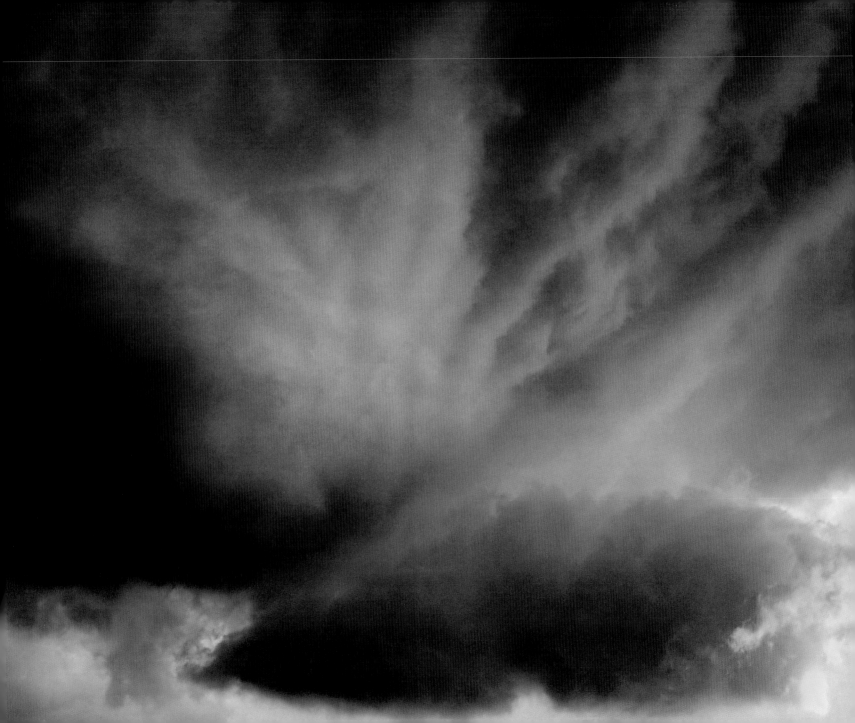

The clouds are racing right at me – passing just overhead – and I'm glued to the spot.

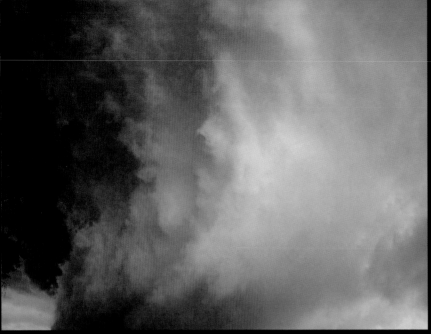

I probably stop too close to the cell, but the setting sun lends the cloud an amazing color and I just want to take it in. The clouds are racing right at me - passing just overhead - and I'm glued to the spot.

Numerous CGs crack from the cloud. This bolt is probably only about a hundred or so meters away.

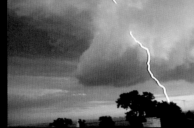 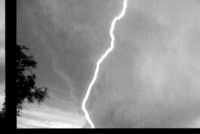

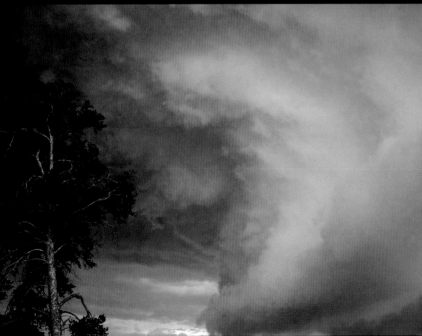

The cell continues to get more surreal as a mid-level funnel on steroids begins to wrap itself around the updraft.

The cell continues to get more surreal as a mid-level funnel on steroids begins to wrap itself around the updraft. Still to this day, I've never witnessed or seen pictures of a detached funnel as big as this.

As the sun slips away, I'm left with one more magical scene. Look how ragged the bottoms of these individual updrafts are as they feed up into the storm with intense convection. Cold air is contaminating the warm air coming into the base, causing the cloud to elevate and eventually die as it blows east.

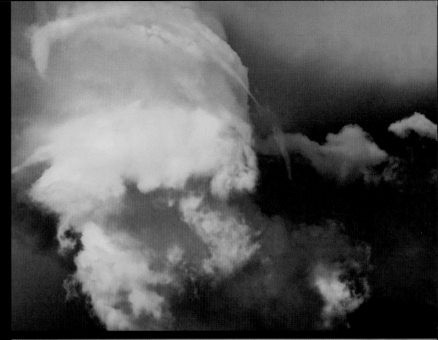

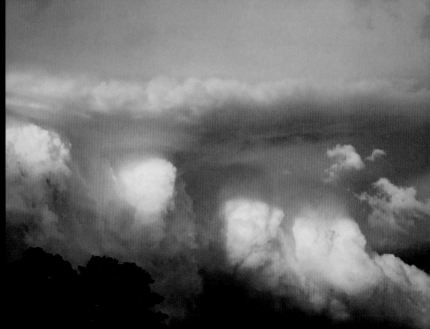

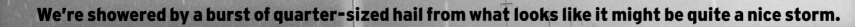
We're showered by a burst of quarter-sized hail from what looks like it might be quite a nice storm.

MOSQUERA, NEW MEXICO

June 3

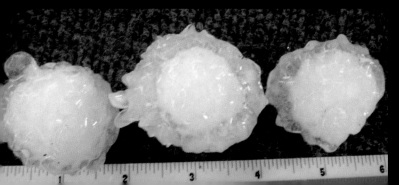

ERIC: June 2003 was one heck of a month for chasing. Jeff Lawson, Scott Blair and I were in northwest New Mexico, where the atmospheric instability remained good for several days and gave us four good days of chasing. The roads around these parts really suck and it's damn cold near the mountains, but the change of scenery was refreshing.

We make our way to the target in northwest New Mexico when we're showered by a burst of quarter-sized hail from what looks like it might be quite a nice storm.

Further down the road we gather some larger, aggressive-looking spiked hail measuring around two inches (5 cm).

Southeast of the storm we get a good view of incredible structure from the top of a ridge.

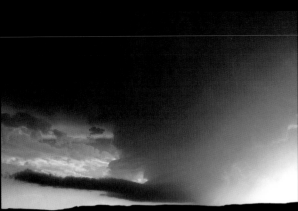

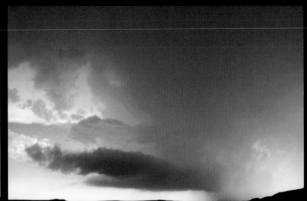

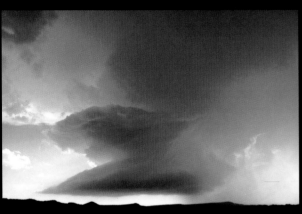

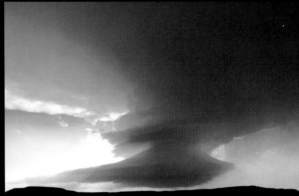

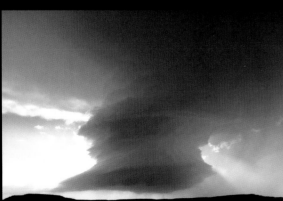

We move off the ridge and head further southeast to get the whole thing into a super wide-angle lens. The precipitation under the storm disappears as it shapes into an amazing low precipitation (LP) structure, with a unique bell-shaped lowering. **The landscapes around this part of New Mexico are stunning** and with nobody else around we have this awesome scene all to ourselves.

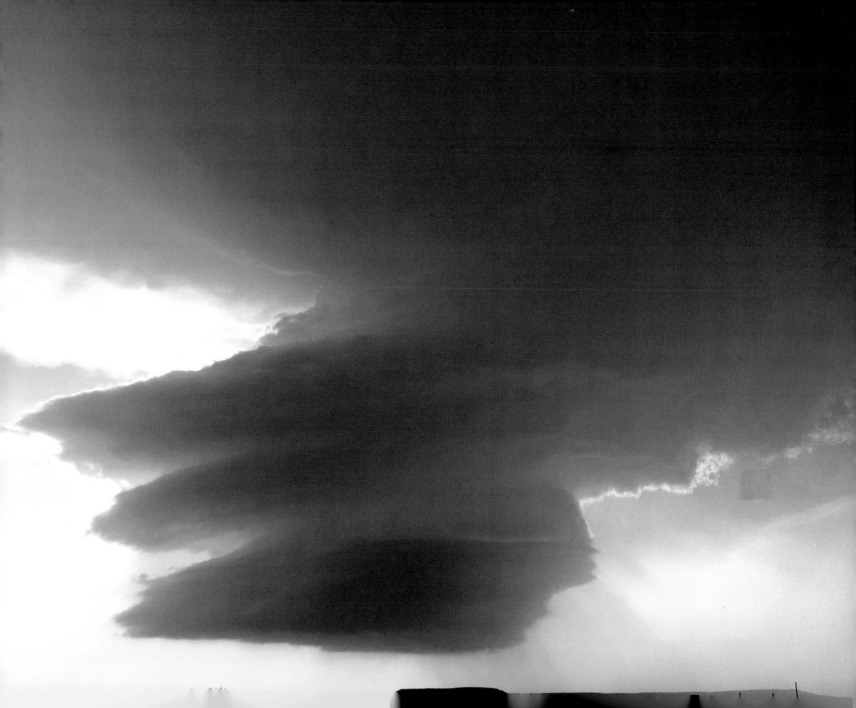

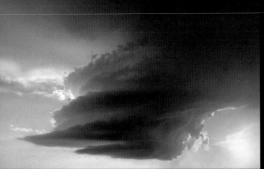
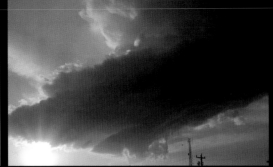
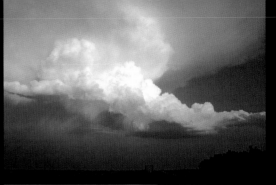
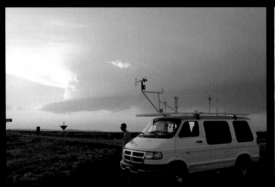
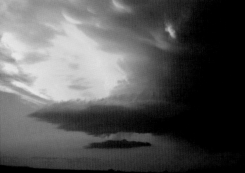
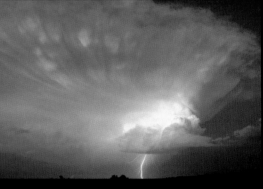

The storm is now drifting slowly, barely moving at all, so we just sit and watch the show as the structure of this rare cell continues to develop. Striations create grooves in the lowering, indicating strong rotation and marking the flow of air at the base, which gives it this unique corkscrew form. It isn't a particularly strong storm, but **the structure sure is satisfying.**

It's still rotating, but gradually weakening and losing organization.

As the first storm disappears, we can see a new structure develop to our north. It is very elevated and weaker than the first, but it looks worth waiting for

We wait for ages to catch lightning and finally capture one of only two bolts from the blue with a long exposure, which rounds off our day of New Mexico LPs handsomely. We'd booked rooms in nearby Tucumcari, but the place looks like a converted prison and the idea of waking up there is just too depressing, so we convince them to give us our money back and retreat to decent lodgings back in Amarillo.

Lovely-looking mammatus
frames the skyscape and becomes
a major feature of the cell.

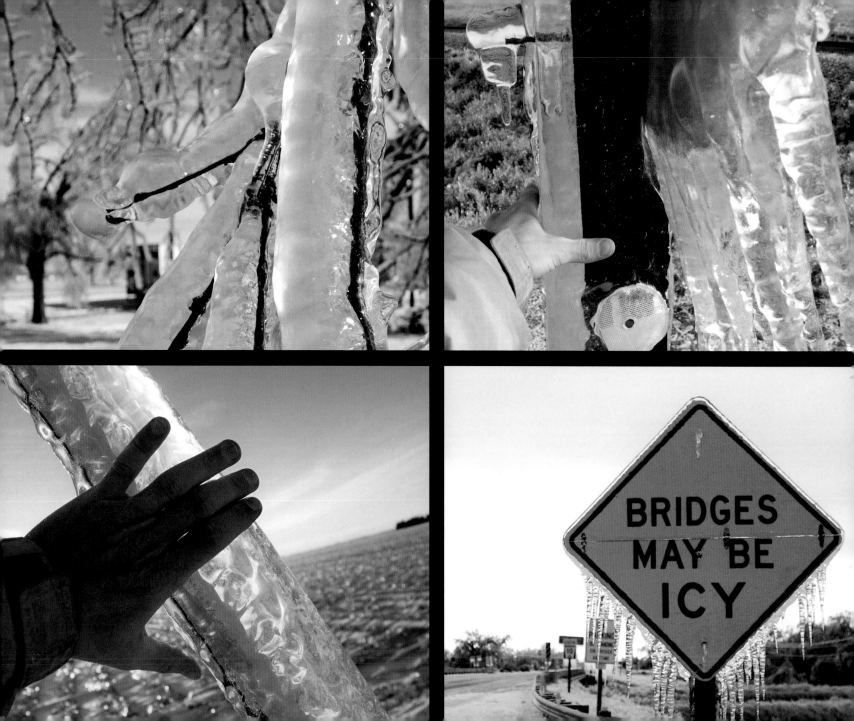

WINTER STORM CHASE AROUND COZAD, NEBRASKA DECEMBER 29-31, 2006

Out of the chase season there are still storms to capture and I really enjoy good snow storms. My corner of Nebraska didn't seem to want to have one this year, so I headed west to view a forecasted snow storm. As I approach my target it starts to sleet hard, so I figure it's best to make sure I can get a room before everyone else. I really don't like the idea of being caught out without a motel room in freezing rain and sleet. The next day I drive around and there is some freezing rain, but it kind of sucks too. Still, the weather becomes more harsh and a very severe ice storm starts, so I stay in the motel again.

The following day it looks like it's all eased off: the sun is shining and the skies are very clear. Time to go home, I suppose. But as I drive home it becomes shocking quite what mother nature can do with a bit of freezing rain. As I get further east, I realize how much thicker the ice has become. There are cars everywhere along the roadside and the roads are becoming slicker. The wind is hitting me and I can feel the back end slide. I stop off at a gas station west of Kearney and find tree branches completely encased in solid ice. It is incredible.

Walking further, with the tall grass cracking as I brush pass, is rather fun. When I first found this place I assumed it was gravel that had frozen, but after kicking down through the surface it turned out that it was a grass field, covered in thick ice. I guess that small pieces of ice had fallen from the trees and frozen up into ice pebbles.

I decide to get out of Kearney because it's just a big mess and too many people are out and about. I need gas, but everywhere is either closed or has huge lines of people waiting, so I head toward Kenesaw, passing more snapped power lines on the roadside. The further I go, the thicker the ice gets. A lot of fences are damaged, so cattle are roaming about and seem a bit confused. A guy is looking at me as if to say "what the hell happened?"

I find this little circus of downed major transmission lines. They are pretty large and made of metal. The scene stays the same for many miles and it isn't just Nebraska - Colorado and Kansas are also badly hit. What I'm seeing as a result of this historic storm is so beautiful, but there is a sad side too: the cost of repairing the damage will surely be tens or hundreds of millions of dollars and for many people it must have been pretty miserable.

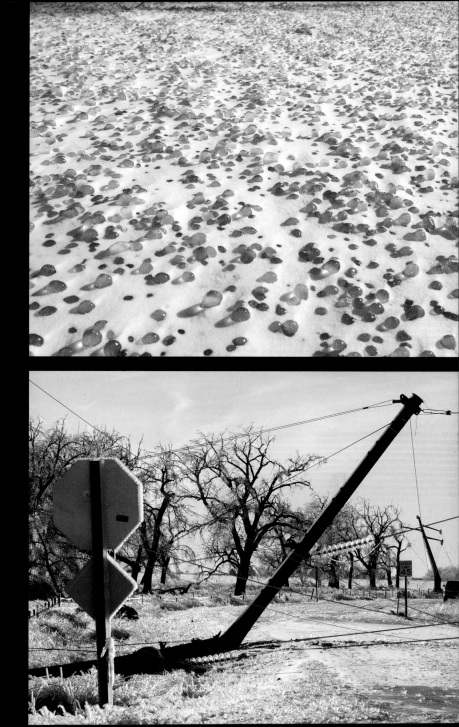

The base starts to show some signs of strong rotation and funnels appear. We damn near missed it.

ATTICA, KANSAS'S
May 29

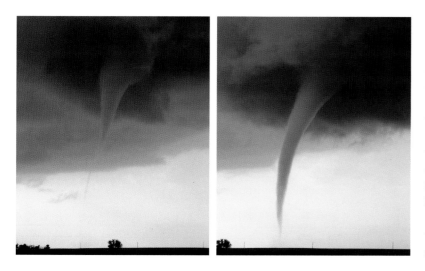

ERIC: Choosing where to target for a chase is the most important decision to make on any day, but with all the forecasting knowledge and experience of storm movement in the world, you're still at the mercy of the gods. Having a gut feeling about a position often doesn't count for much, so all the time you're looking for alternatives and new options. On this day we'd spent two hours looking into the Kansas sky, wondering if anything would happen, while all the time radar showed tornadic storms raging to our north and south, all over a three-state area. The nearest was a monster of a storm near Oklahoma City, about 100 miles away, which was doable, but Murphy's Law was bound to apply: the minute we left, all hell would break loose where we'd been waiting. As it turns out, not much happened to that Oklahoma City monster and our patience was rewarded, but it's luck more than anything else.

After hours of sitting there, waiting, deliberating, and on the verge of leaving for a new target, an RFD cut becomes visible on our storm, the base starts to show some signs of strong rotation and funnels appear. We damn near missed it.

A thin funnel forms from the base of the rotation north of us, so **we jump into the car and speed toward it, stop on a quiet dirt road and run into a farmer's field to get the best sight of it**. As soon as I am ready to shoot, the funnel majestically reaches out of the base and **touches down for the first time**.

When it hits, the sun illuminates the base of the tornado, giving it a golden tip, and a significant debris cloud emerges as hay bales explode in the fields it was chewing up. Quite often when there is a storm active nearby, the air fills with the sound of wind, but **this is quite a surreal scene – it's deadly silent and you can hear birds chirping away**. If it wasn't for the sight of this thing whirling away in the distance you wouldn't have thought there was anything strange in the atmosphere.

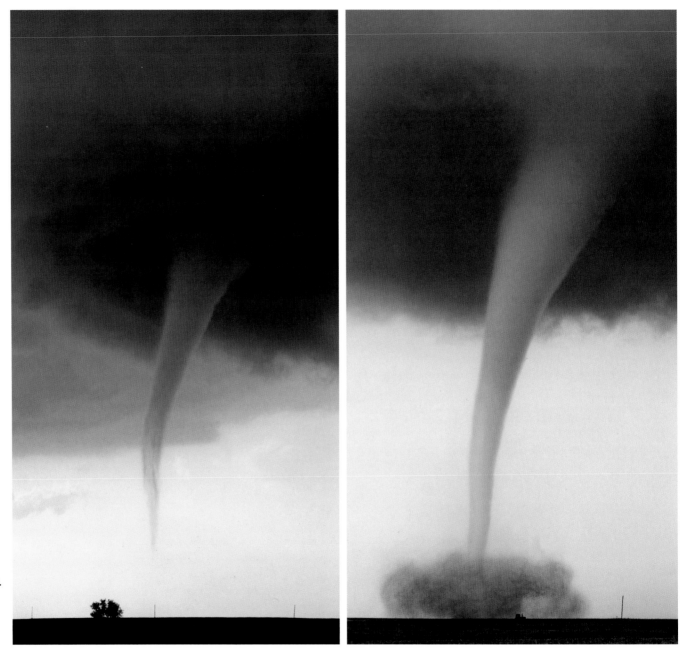

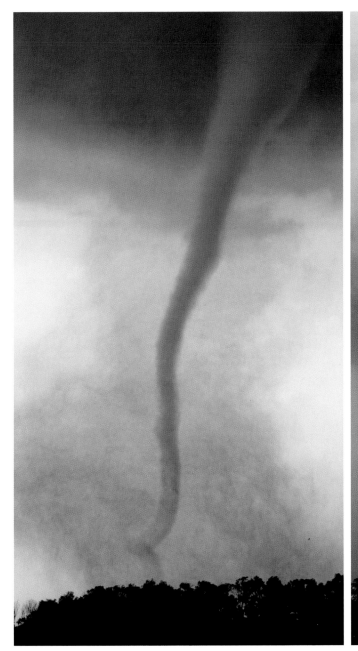
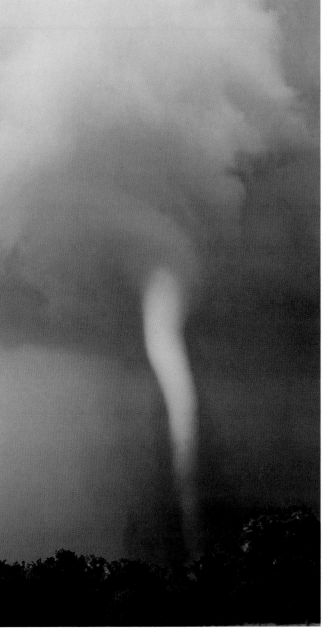

The tornado keeps going with intense motion at ground level: way longer than we'd expected. It's moving exceptionally slowly – first toward the northeast and then it seems to spin in place a while before drifting slowly westward. The funnel has several kinks as it crosses trees and the force of tearing up the vegetation disrupts the clean lines of the tapered structure.

The debris cloud adopts a strange hue as **the tornado whips up the red Kansas dirt**.

Whatever it is, it's pretty big and flies out of the funnel at high speed.

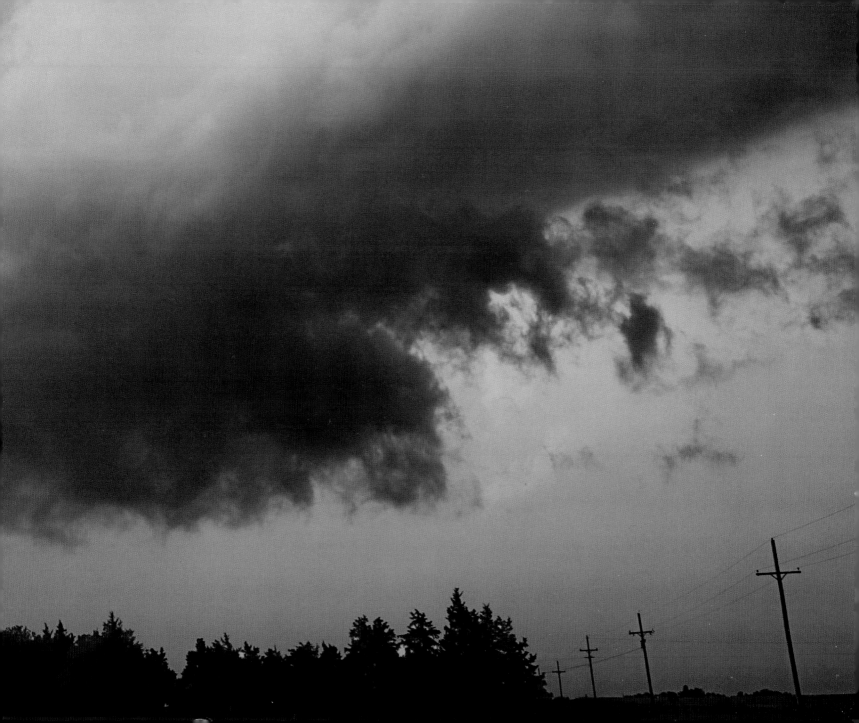

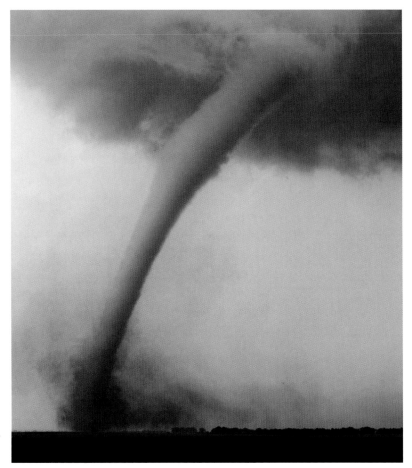

We want to keep on top of this tornado so we follow it east, but it's becoming like a video game, with the storm throwing obstacles in our path. First a bridge over the river is closed due to the danger, so we have to track back west, and then we're stopped cold by downed power lines near Crystal Springs. **The structure has become quite stunning** and as we take in this wider view the updraft completely occludes, leaving the tornado to rope out and show the force of the rotation, which looks like rings along the shaft of the funnel.

It continues to show terrific shape and is clearly very intense at the ground. On the left side of the tornado you can see a dot that we think is a tree - or at least a big chunk of one - but can't quite tell. Whatever it is, it's pretty big and flies out of the funnel at high speed.

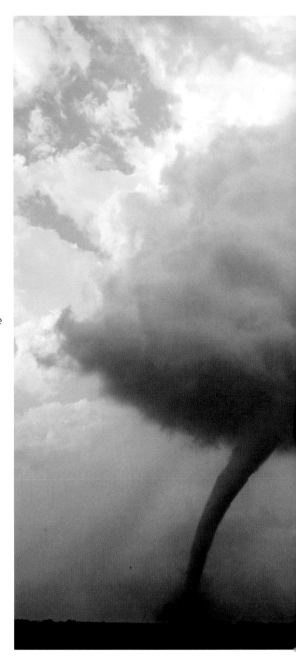

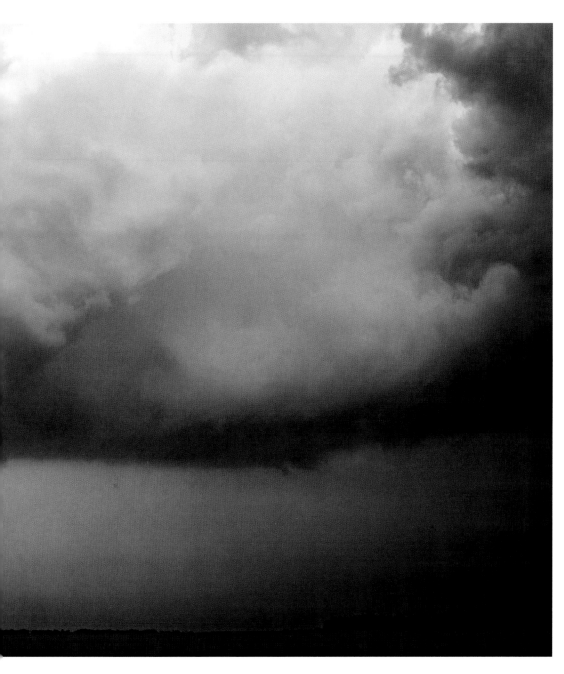

Finally it completely dissipates into a needle in front of the blue sky before vanishing. **It had been on the ground for 24 minutes** and we were pleased to have caught pretty much all of it before we ran out of road.

With barely enough time to catch our breath, **we notice a new tornado** to our southeast and possibly one to our north, which must have both developed as the first one died.

We get within two miles of the new tornado, by which time it has grown significantly into a dusty wedge. **We don't want to get held up by the debris** and we race east toward the town of Argonia, to get a good vantage point.

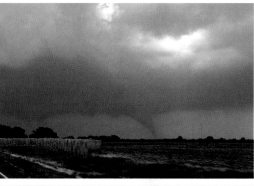

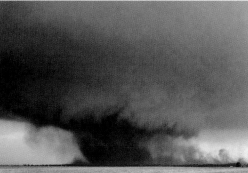

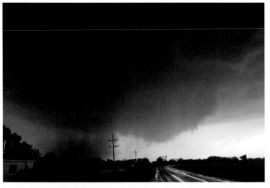
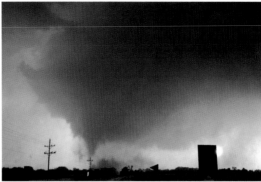
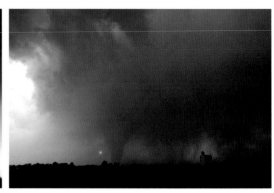
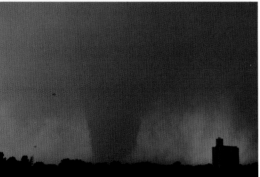
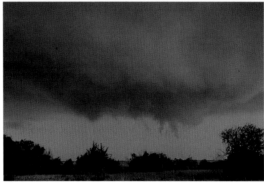

Closer to the town, the tornado lifts up, but then starts to reorganize.

Before long the tornado develops into a large cylinder shape. We leave to pursue another tornado half a mile to our east. The image on the far left was taken at 0121 UTC looking almost due east as the tornado moves northward. It is about 1.5 miles away and just west of Argonia. The tornado grew into a wedge-shaped tornado as it slowly moved northward wrapping in rain at 0130 UTC, northeast of Argonia. It eventually dissipated at 0149 UTC. This puts the life of the tornado at over 52 minutes, probably closer to 60.

Pretty quickly it turns into a large cylinder shape in the distance, but gradually wraps up in rain, obscuring the view.

Suddenly we're blown around in a crazy wind event as a new tornado forms above us. It's only just organizing, so it isn't that strong, but it sure makes us a little nervous at first.

Suddenly we're blown around in a crazy wind event as a new tornado forms above us.

We turn to follow this new tornado, which touches down. There isn't a soul around, so **I call 911** frequently to let them know the movements **in case it becomes a threat to nearby towns**.

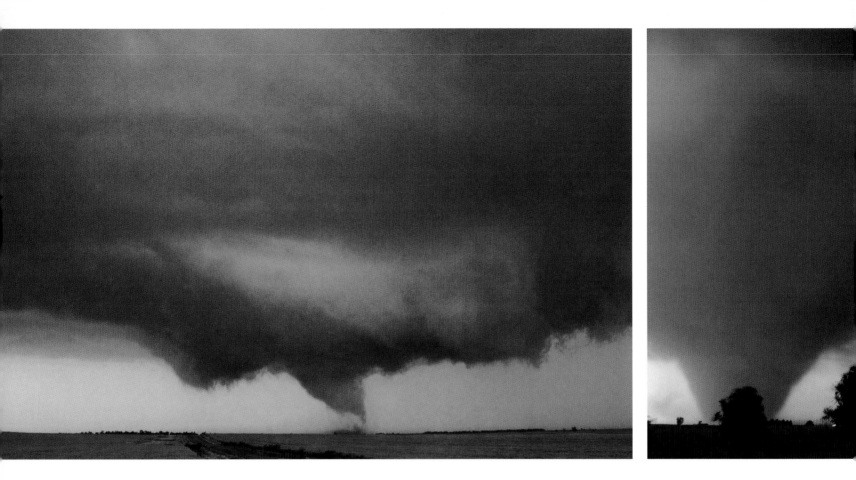

Our current tornado ropes out and dies just as a new one appears and grows into a wedge in the distance. It's all a little confusing and we're not sure which way to go!

We'd seen some terrific tornado shapes and were lucky the storm had been moving so slowly.

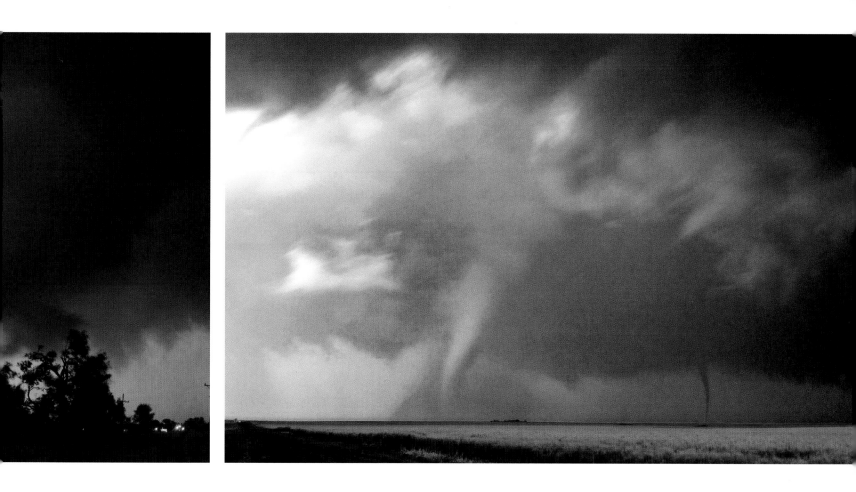

As the fourth tornado begins to weaken and turns into this stove-pipe shape a fifth tornado fires and touches down at the same time! You can see the thin funnel back there in the distance. Having two tornadoes on the ground at the same time is a rare sight and reminds me why I love chasing storms so much. It was getting too dark to really capture events, so we decide to call it a day. We'd seen some terrific tornado shapes and were lucky the storm had been moving so slowly, enabling us to catch so much of the action. On the way back we realized that these towns had had a brush with some nasty tornadoes just two weeks earlier, so I guess they were less pleased with today's weather.

It's strange how warnings to stay away from an area are exactly what will attract people like me!

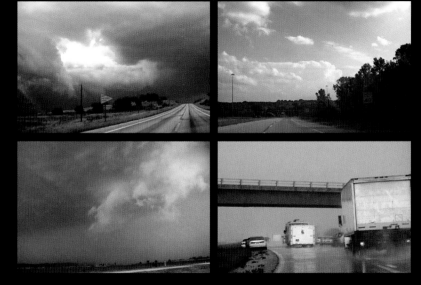

MIKE: Coming very late in the season, my last supercell of the year was exceptionally good for Iowa in August, and a great way to close 2004.

As I head toward southwest Iowa to track two supercells that had appeared on the radar, channel six in Omaha reports 100 mph winds, and then tornado warnings for the region I was heading to. I guess it's strange how warnings to stay away from an area are exactly what will attract people like me!

Further south I get my first look at the base of the left split, moving left, away from the more southern storm. Entering the core of the storms, I keep the video camera rolling. Approaching Nebraska City, on the border with Iowa, the interstate gets a whole lot more dangerous: people were just stopping on the interstate under bridges to avoid hail and, I guess, trying to work out what to do. I can't work out which way the meso and lowering are heading and I really don't want to drive into the back of it, but figure I surely am.

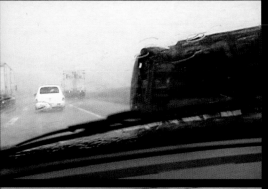

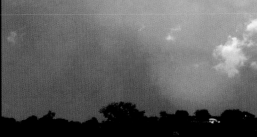

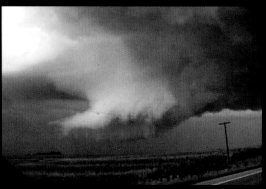

The wind is getting really intense now. This video capture makes the visibility look a lot better than it actually was because I was being shielded by a truck to my left – I couldn't see the semi that had been pushed over by the wind until I was right on it. **The traffic was generally very erratic and I didn't enjoy the road at all.** I called 911 to make sure emergency vehicles were on the way to the semi, which they were, and, as far as I know, nobody was hurt.

Once past the interstate traffic, I'm in the hilly terrain around the extreme southwest corner of Iowa. **I love to drive on these roads where you get a cool rollercoaster feeling at every hilltop.** I see the cell produce a tornado that touches down while I'm on the crest of a hill, but between the peaks and troughs of the hills I can't get a proper view of it.

Looking east, I can see a new meso with a very strong RFD cut.

A tornado forms in the distance, but soon ropes out and dies.

A well-defined lowering appears and is rotating as hard as anything I've ever seen. **Time to pull over and get some proper shots.**

The storm clearly had a lot of strength and I can't believe it didn't produce a tornado right there and then. It didn't, but still, **watching this thing take shape was incredible.**

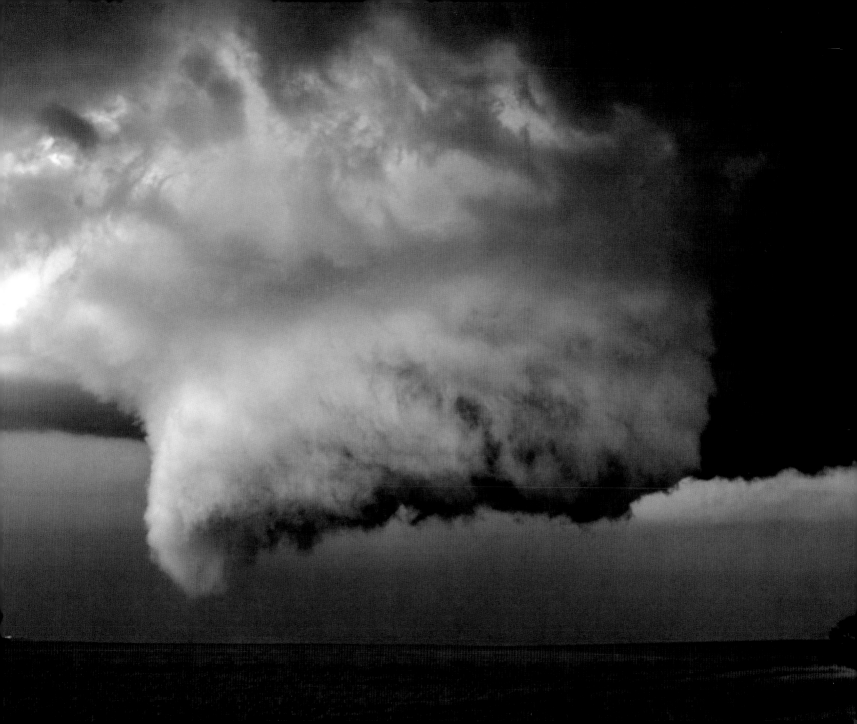

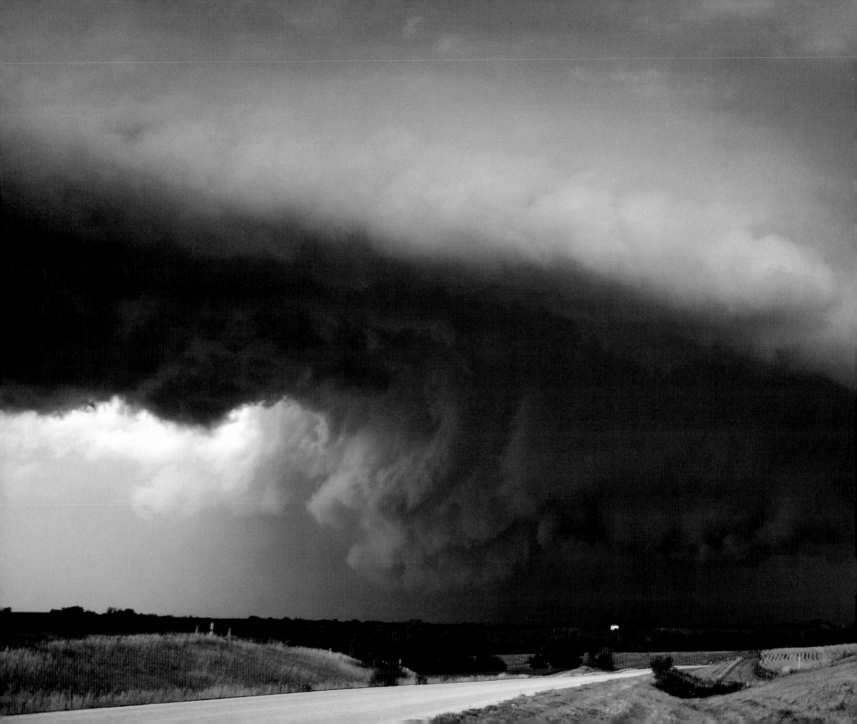

The cell continues to morph into incredible structure and you can see a strong beaver's tail that has formed.

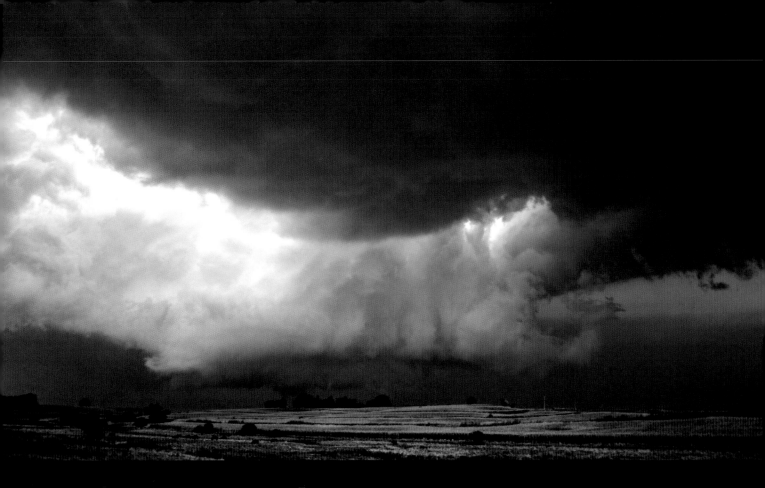

Here I'm looking due north at the lowering, which is behind intense RFD that has a pretty cold look to it. The clouds moving south are probably travelling at nearly 100 mph.

The rotation is still very strong and multiple vortices dance around beneath the bowl. Tornado activity from this storm damaged several homes, some severely, in the area.

Tornado activity from this storm damaged several homes, some severely, in the area.

**The road options around this storm were leading me
all over the countryside, first east and finally northeast.**
Despite still being tornado warned in the area, the cell
is becoming too undercut and linear in appearance.
Heading home, I catch some nice CGs from the dispersing
storm as it darkened. I think **the day must have sent the
wildlife a little crazy** - two deer and a dog jumped out in
front of me on the way home, but thankfully I avoided them.

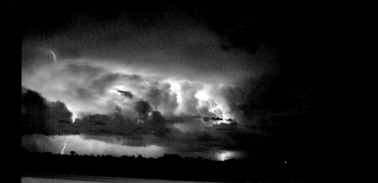

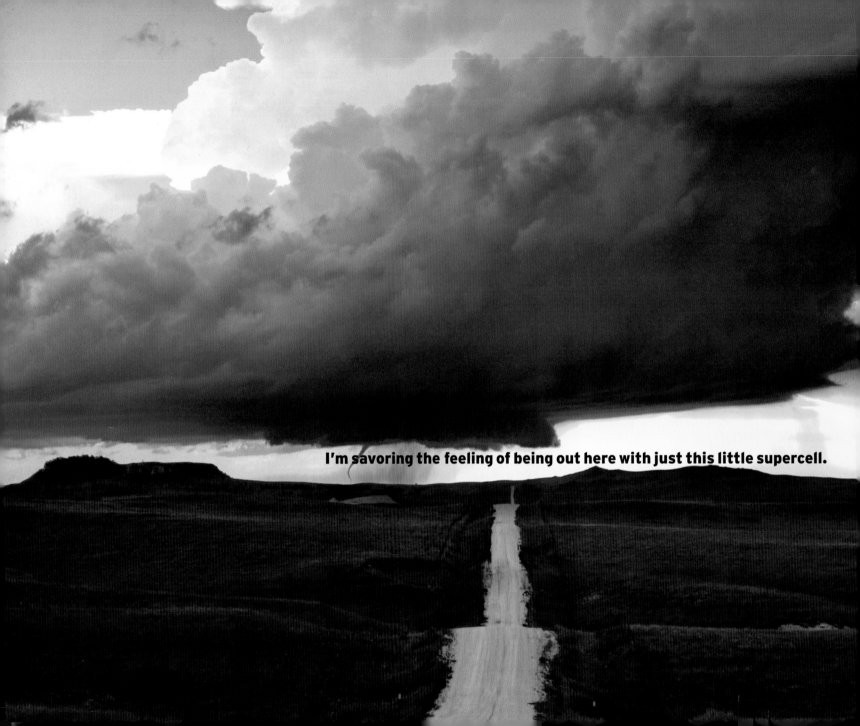

I'm savoring the feeling of being out here with just this little supercell.

MURDO, SOUTH DAKOTA
June 7

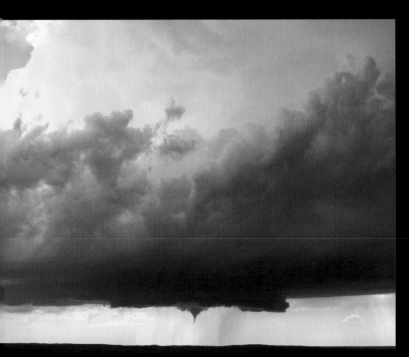

MIKE: Here I was, alone, near the Badlands of South Dakota, jumping up and down and screaming at a storm cloud miles away. I'd found this little guy early on and had watched and watched as it struggled. There had been some signs of the precipitation, but they disappeared to virtually nothing. Giving the cloud hell seemed to be the only thing to do. It must have worked: pretty quickly a new plume came up at the back of the cell and I was filled with hope.

I'm savoring the feeling of being out here with just this little supercell; there isn't a building in sight and I haven't seen a soul for hours. As the cell clears a large rock formation, **I catch a glimpse of a rope-shaped tornado descending. My first of the year – what a great feeling!**

ERIC: Boy, was I exhausted on this chase. I'd started out in Texas at about 9 pm the night before and made it to a motel in Nebraska about 5 am. Not surprisingly, I overslept and was on the edge of my seat for the six-hour drive north, keeping an eye on the satellite as the weather took shape up there.

As I get closer I feel comforted when I start to hear chaser chatter over the radio. I catch the action just in time, and run into Amos Magliocco, Scott Blair, and Scott Currens, who I get to enjoy the day's storms with.

A funnel forms at the base, which briefly touches down as a debris cloud followed by a roping tornado. I'm not really expecting it since the cell is so high based and low precipitation, so it's a real nice surprise. As the tornado weakens, the storm seems to launch into a new gear, speeding up rapidly to take a fresh shape.

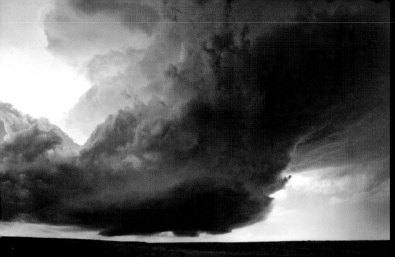

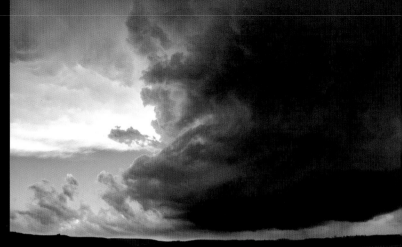

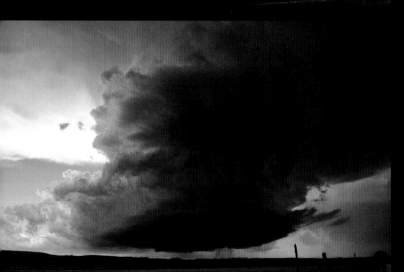

MIKE: Moving to the northeast of the cell, toward Kadoka, there's mammatus forming to the left side of the cloud and the core is beginning to really pick up on the radar. **I'm getting hailed on, but it's tame compared to the baseball-sized hail reported in Kadoka**: the big stuff is on my heels, though, as I glide east with the storm.

The big stuff is on my heels, though, as I glide east with the storm.

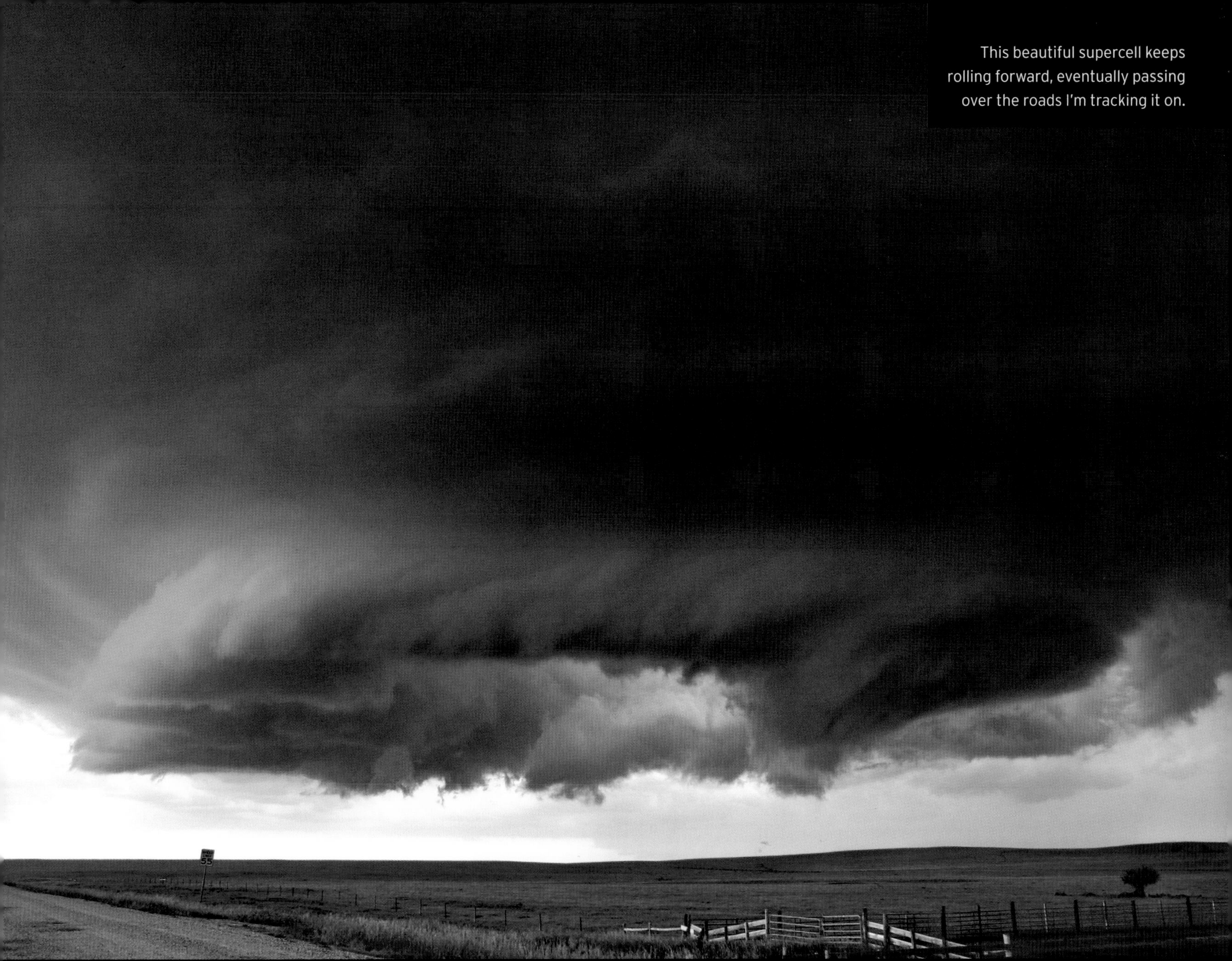

This beautiful supercell keeps rolling forward, eventually passing over the roads I'm tracking it on.

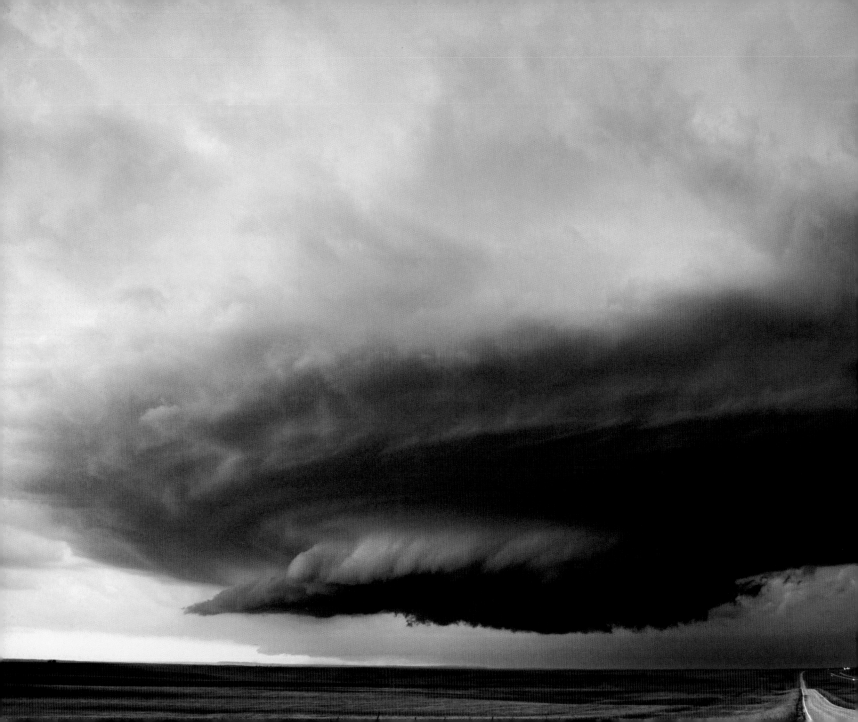

This new meso has me zigzagging northeast. What structure!

ERIC: Looking north as we drive through the Badlands National Park, a long funnel develops from an old occluded meso, but **nobody is close enough to know if it ever touches down.**

A new wall cloud is set in motion to our east.

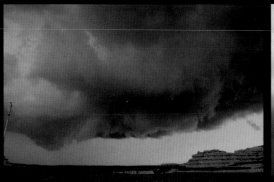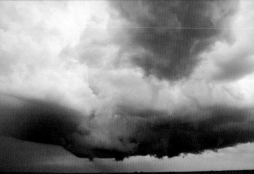

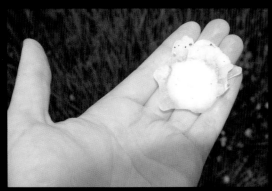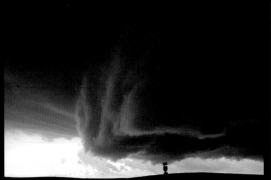

I stop off quickly to pick up some hail with spikes that had fallen around 20 minutes earlier.

The storm drifts over no man's land without offering many road options, so we drive underneath the wall cloud and **struggle to flank the storm path**.

As we catch up with the new heavily rotating cell, Amos finds signs for an old ghost town called Okaton which we figure will be a great setting for the passing storm, and find a big abandoned grain elevator in the foreground.

You don't see these little swirls on the side of cells very often. They're called Kelvin-Helmholtz vortices (we call them "Eddies") and they are absolutely beautiful: the real highlight of the action in the sky today.

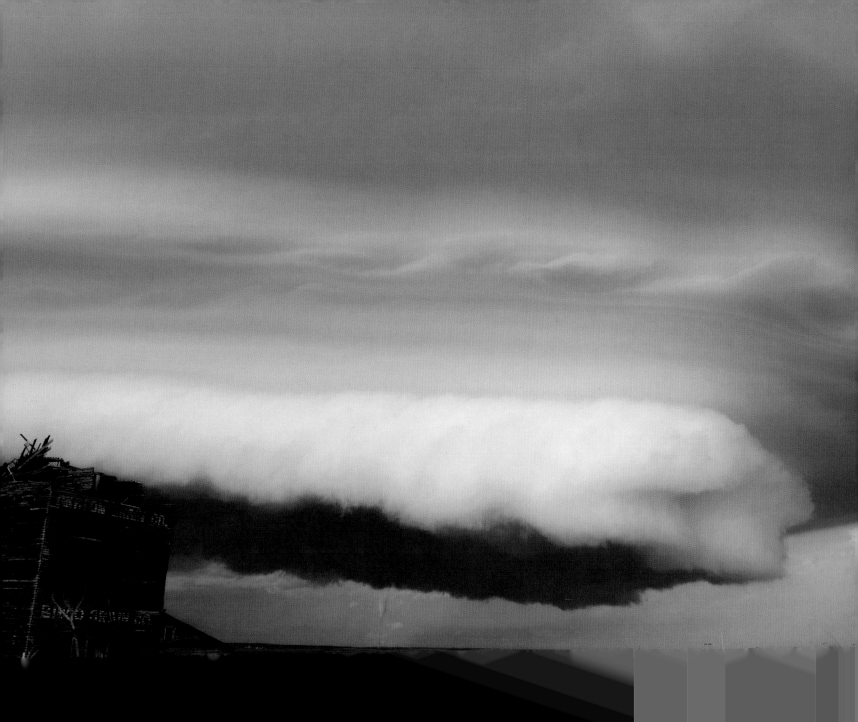

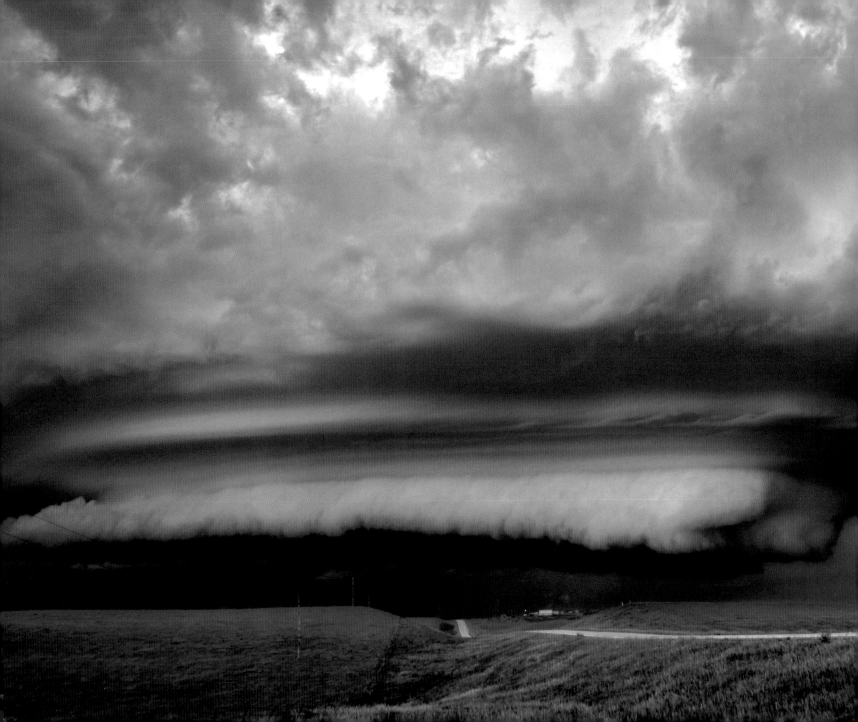

MIKE: This new meso has me zigzagging northeast. What structure!

Perhaps I should have raced east to catch the ongoing structure, but it's dark and getting late, so I sit it out in a tiny town called Murdo and shoot some video. **Here she comes!**

I can't figure out what this guy is doing, pumping gas and not getting back in the car as the storm pounds the town.

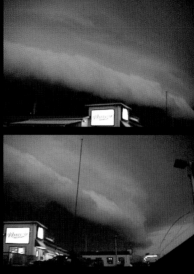

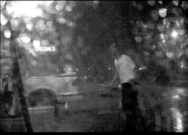

ERIC: It's getting late and we're satisfied that we've caught the best of it, plus I'm ready to drop. There's shelter nearby so we decide to let the gust front hit us and grab a hail burger in a place next to the gas station in Murdo.

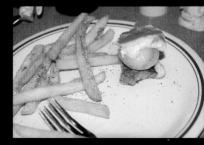

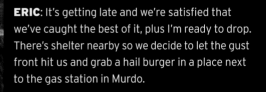

173

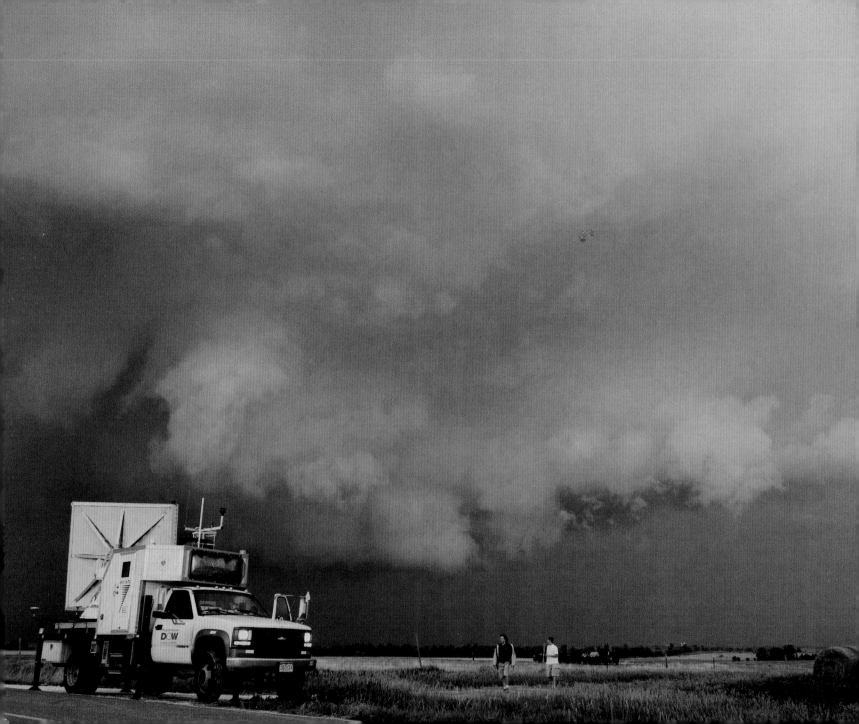

...ion of chasing is forecasting, and you can't catch storms successfully without putting the groundwork into understanding and following the weather patterns well in advance. Chasing isn't cheap - gas, hotels, food, oil, tires...the list goes on, but a bad forecast is more than just time and money wasted - the real cost is the aggravation of missing a good storm.

The main ingredients that chasers look for that will lead to supercell thunderstorms are sufficient vertical wind shear, instability, and a form of lift to initiate convection. Every chaser has their own technique for forecasting severe storms and there is no simple formula to get it right consistently, but with time you develop a process that you become comfortable with while still learning new tricks and patterns. Most of the data we use comes from government websites such as NOAA and the Storm Prediction Center. I start by examining large-scale synoptic features in the mid and upper levels and work my way down to the surface, where mesoscale features come into play. Forecasting can start as early as a week before the event and as time draws closer, a region can be chosen with the best chance of violent storms.

Sometimes, if the target area is too far to reach on the morning of the event, I'll drive to the area the night before and book into a motel so that I can make an early start. The morning before an event is the most fun - I have a mixture of excitement and butterflies in anticipation of what the day might bring while I'm checking the early weather ...t my initial path toward the storm.

The internet. Obviously a crucial tool for chasing when forecasting storms, but the laptop remains important throughout the chase. From plugging into the connection at the motel to taking advantage of WiFi hotspots throughout the plains, it allows us to keep an eye on the storm trends with radar data that updates every six minutes and refine our target, as well as track our location with GPS data. Years ago chasers used paper maps to navigate themselves around Tornado Alley, but thankfully these days we don't have that headache. GPS (Global Positioning System) mapping is by far the most important chasing tool I have. Often you're in the middle of nowhere, on unfamiliar parts of the plains and roads that are always unpredictable. The most dangerous part of chasing, more than anything the storm is going to throw at you, is the driving, especially when your focus is firmly on the sky. GPS allows me to plan my route safely: either toward the part of the storm I want to witness or an escape route to avoid strong winds or tornadoes.

Another vital piece of equipment is the XM weather receiver, which gives us severe weather and tornado warnings and can indicate where the tornadic portion of a thunderstorm is located.

Weather instruments mounted on the roof of my vehicle augment my laptop data. These allow me to monitor real-time pressure, dewpoint, and wind data, which is stored on a datalogger for use later and displayed as graphs on a handheld unit. I pay very close attention to the wind speeds and report severe wind informati...n to the relev...t authorities.

I have a ham radio installed in the vehicle. This is used to contact other chasers as well as report severe weather through ham radio skywarn nets, and when we can't communicate through the radio we switch to cell phones.

Of course, all of this equipment for forecasting and measuring the storm environment is key to my chase, but I'm there to document my observations, so I never leave without my Canon D60 digital SLR camera.

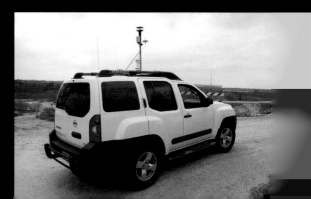

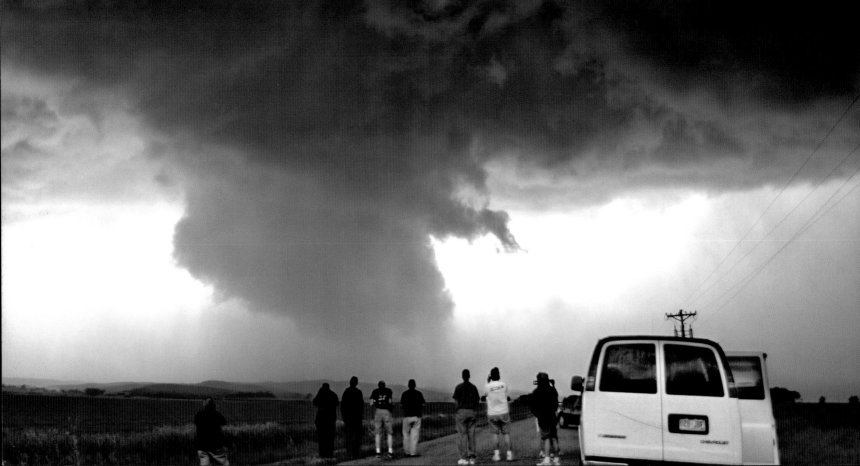

THE
SCIENCE
OF
STORMS

BY CHUCK DOSWELL

INTRODUCTION

My goal with this discussion is not to teach meteorology, which requires a lot of math and physics to understand properly, but to explain what Mike and Eric's images reveal. What is creating these cloud formations? Why do some storms produce really violent weather compared to most thunderstorms? Do the spectacular cloud formations tell us what to expect with the weather?

WHY ARE THERE THUNDERSTORMS?

In order to understand the causes of thunderstorms, we must begin with some basic ideas about how the atmosphere produces weather in the first place. The most important notion is that virtually all of the world's weather is tied to the fact that the incoming energy from the sun is not evenly distributed. In the tropics, the sun is almost directly overhead throughout the year, whereas in the polar regions the sun doesn't shine at all for months during the winter, and even though the days are long during polar summers, the sun remains fairly low on the horizon. Therefore, the polar regions remain cold relative to the tropics. In the *mid-latitudes*, i.e., neither the tropics nor the polar regions, low sun angles occur in the winter, with short days, and high sun angles in the summer, with long days. This produces the seasonal temperature differences in mid-latitudes.

Given that the tropics remains warm virtually all year round, the differences in solar heating result in a cycle during the year: the temperature difference from the polar regions to the tropics is at its highest during the mid-to-late winter and at its smallest in the mid-to-late summer. This temperature difference, in turn, is the main driving force for the so-called jet streams in the upper atmosphere (at a height of about 10 miles or so). These high-speed *rivers* of wind above the surface are a critical factor in storms, as I will explain later. Upper-level jet streams are strongest and closest to the tropics during the winter. During the summer, jet streams are weakest and closest to the polar regions.

In the transition seasons of spring and fall, the jet streams may be weaker than in winter, but are stronger than in summer. It is during the transition seasons that severe thunderstorms are most likely. In the United States, spring is typically much more active than fall. This lack of symmetry is associated with the accumulated effect of all the thunderstorms during the spring and summer, which act eventually to make the atmosphere more stable in the fall than in the spring.

One by-product of the temperature difference between the tropics and the poles is the so-called extratropical cyclone (ETC). This low-pressure system is often seen on TV weather maps. Fig. 1 shows a false-color satellite view of three ETCs across the United States: ETCs draw their energy from the temperature difference between the tropics and the poles, and in the Northern Hemisphere, rotate counter clockwise in response to the rotation of the earth. Their rotation produces winds that draw warm air from the south and bring it poleward, while at the same time drawing cold air from the north, bringing it equatorward. This large-scale airflow is the atmosphere's way of reducing the temperature difference between the tropics and the poles. The amount of heat transported by ETCs is vast.

The sun also heats the surface of the earth. On land, this heating produces what is known as the "sensible" heat in the atmosphere in contact with the ground. Sensible heat can be measured directly with a thermometer. However, when the sun heats the oceans part of that heat raises the temperature of the water, while it also contributes to the evaporation of the water. As anyone who has stepped out of the shower knows, evaporating water absorbs heat – it makes us feel cold until we towel off the water. This heat remains with the evaporated water, which is transformed to a colorless, odorless gas called water vapor which is mixed with the air. The heat that

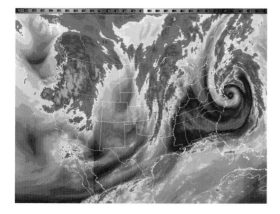

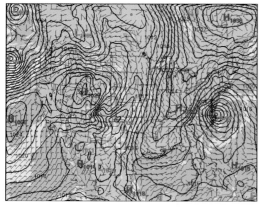

Fig. 1: False-color image of three ETCs: one entering the Pacific northwestern USA, the second moving through the central plains, and a third just off the east coast.

Fig. 2: Surface weather map, showing the surface winds and pressures associated with the three ETCs shown in fig. 1. Wind barbs indicate the speed and direction of the airflow, which is counterclockwise around the low-pressure centers (red "L" symbols) and clockwise around the high-pressure centers (blue "H" symbols).

water vapor contains is called latent heat and can't be measured with a thermometer, but is revealed in the air's humidity. The more water vapor the air contains, the higher its humidity. The water vapor content of the air is a critical factor in the development of thunderstorms.

The sun deposits most of its energy at the surface of the earth, so both the sensible heat and the latent heat accumulate at relatively low levels. This effect is evidently strongest during the summer, weakest during the winter, and is somewhere in between in the transition seasons of spring and fall. When there is an excess of heat at low levels, which is similar to what happens with the water in a pan set on a stove burner, the heat excess at low levels wants to make the air overturn, to distribute that excess of heat at low levels upward.

This produces rising currents of air, sometimes called thermals, which carry excess heat from low levels upward. In between the thermals, currents of air descend, bringing cooler air downward to replace the heated air rising in the thermals. The result, on a day with some moisture in the air, is *fair weather cumulus* clouds. These clouds reveal the tops of rising warm thermals while, in between, the cooler air is sinking closer to the surface, to be heated in its turn by the sun's energy. In the process the excess heat is redistributed upward into the atmosphere.

Under the right circumstances, however, this fair-weather response is simply not sufficient to redistribute the low-level sensible and latent heat excess fast enough. Under such conditions, something much stronger than fair-weather cumulus clouds is needed: a thunderstorm.

A simple model of a thunderstorm is given in fig. 3. Such a storm begins with a so-called *towering cumulus* cloud, which is dominated by rising motion (*updraft*).

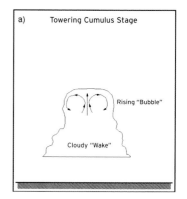

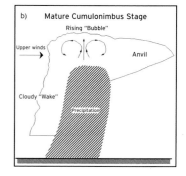

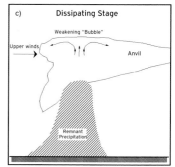

Figs 3 a, b, c: The three stages in the life-cycle of a thunderstorm "cell": the towering cumulus stage, the mature thunderstorm stage, and the dissipating stage.

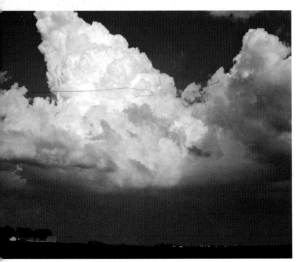

Towering cumulus cloud (TCU)

When air rises in the atmosphere, it is moving from high pressure near the surface to lower pressure aloft. Generally, pressure decreases upward because the earth's gravity causes the air to be most dense near the ground, with that density decreasing upward. As air rises, it expands because the surrounding pressure is reduced. This expansion results in cooling, in the same way that gas coming from a spray can expands and cools, causing the can itself to feel cool to the touch. As air rises in the updraft, air at low levels flows inward to replace it: this is called the *inflow*. The cooling from expansion eventually causes any water vapor the air contains to condense – like a glass of ice water causes water vapor to condense on it – thereby releasing its latent heat. The base of the TCU marks the level where condensation begins in that column of rising air. Latent heat release within the cloud results in temperatures at any level in the cloud being higher than in the surrounding air. Like a hot air balloon, a TCU is *buoyant*.

The next stage is the so-called *mature thunderstorm* (fig. 3b), which includes both strong rising motion and strong sinking motion (*updraft* and *downdraft*) and now precipitation begins. The precipitation is the result of condensation of the water vapor in the rising air – precipitation particles become large enough within the cloud to begin to collect other particles in a process called *coalescence*, eventually growing large enough to fall out of the cloud. The descending precipitation drags the surrounding air downward with it, beginning the downdraft. When some of that precipitation falls into dry air, the condensed water begins to evaporate, which cools the downdraft air, allowing it to be negatively buoyant and enhancing the downdraft in the process.

As the downdraft strikes the surface of the earth, it spreads out, forming the storm's *outflow*, with a miniature version of a cold front, which is called a *gust front*, at the leading edge of the outflow. A mature thunderstorm has both inflow and outflow. Since the outflow is typically cool and moist, it has high humidity and sometimes clouds can form very close to the ground near the gust front, called *scud* clouds. They are generally ragged and turbulent, characteristic of outflow, whereas a thunderstorm's inflow is fairly smooth and produces a reasonably uniform cloud base.

As the rising air ascends, it eventually rises to its *equilibrium level* (EL), where the temperature in the rising air is about the same as the surrounding air. Further ascent produces what is called an *overshooting top*, which becomes negatively buoyant and sinks back down to the EL and then spreads out, forming the so-called thunderstorm *anvil*. Although the height of the EL can vary from case to case, usually it is at a height of 8 to 10 miles, where the upper winds can be strong, carrying the anvil downstream with the upper-level airflow. This anvil cloud spreads both downstream in the winds and outward from the center of the updrafts.

Later in the lifecycle, the updraft portion of the storm weakens and dies, while the precipitation continues to fall out. At this time, the storm is dominated by downdrafts and outflow, which continue for some time. This is called the dissipating stage of the thunderstorm cell (fig. 3c). The precipitation formed within the cell can fall out for several minutes after the clouds have dissipated.

The whole lifecycle of a thunderstorm cell is about 20–40 minutes, around the time that air takes to rise from near the surface to the top of the storm.

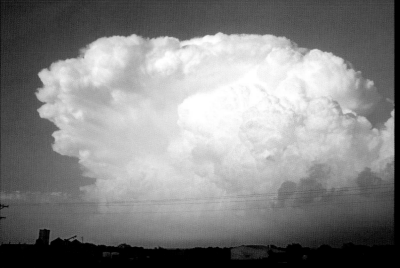

Cumulonimbus cloud

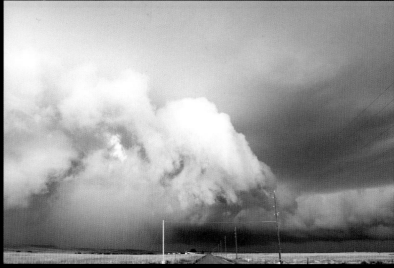

Outflow

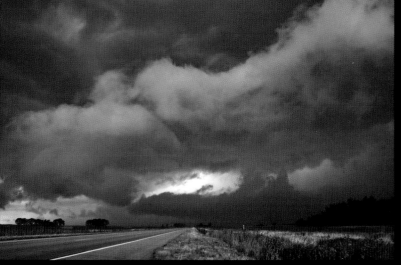

Scud clouds

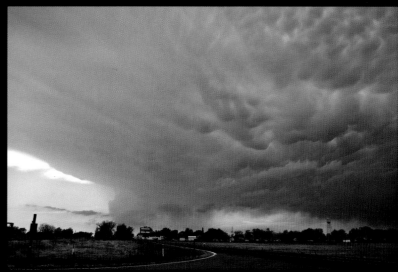

Anvil

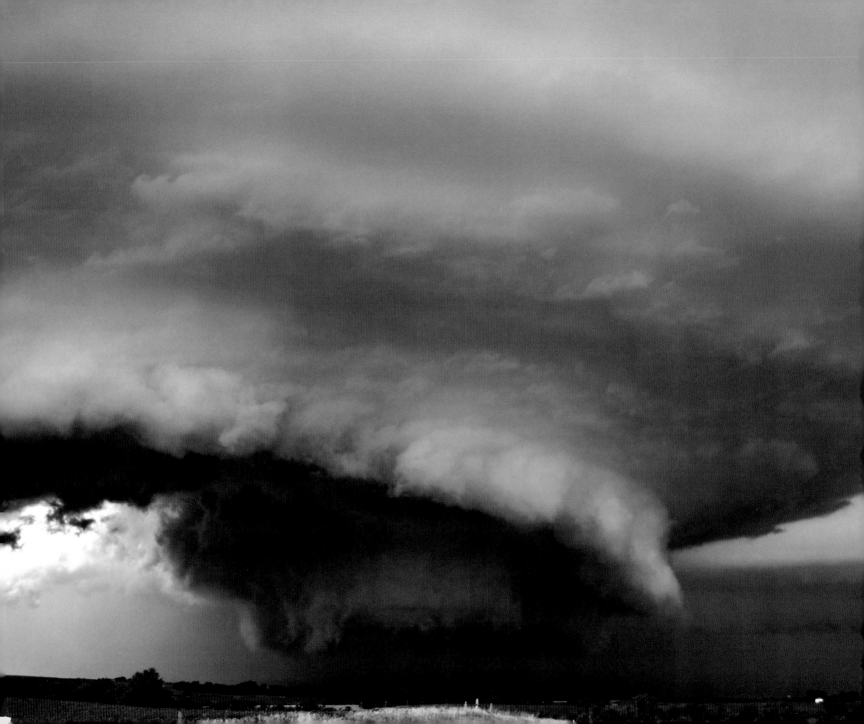

Most thunderstorms last longer than 20 to 40 minutes, so they are composed of more than one such cell. Sometimes there are clusters of cells, each at various stages in their lifecycles. Frequently, the thunderstorm cells are arranged in lines.

SEVERE THUNDERSTORMS

Officially a thunderstorm is called severe if it produces one or more of the following: hailstone with diameters of ¾ inch (2 cm) or more, winds of 58 mph or stronger, or a tornado.

Generally speaking, thunderstorms become severe when they produce a strong updraft, which promotes the production of large hail, a strong downdraft, which increases the speed of the outflow at the surface, or if they rotate, which transforms the thunderstorm from an ordinary storm to a *supercell* storm. The processes that create strong updrafts are not necessarily the same as those that enhance downdrafts, so it is possible that a storm could produce very strong outflow and yet have a relatively weak updraft. Similarly, a strong updraft is not always accompanied by strong downdrafts. Some storms have both strong updrafts and strong downdrafts, and these can produce all forms of severe weather, including heavy rainfall, which although not considered severe in official terms, is still an important type of thunderstorm.

Hailstorms

Hail is necessarily associated with intense updrafts. Particles of ice can grow into large hailstones by being held aloft in the part of the storm where hailstone growth is promoted. This is in a region between the melting level at 0° Celsius (32° Fahrenheit) and the level in the cloud

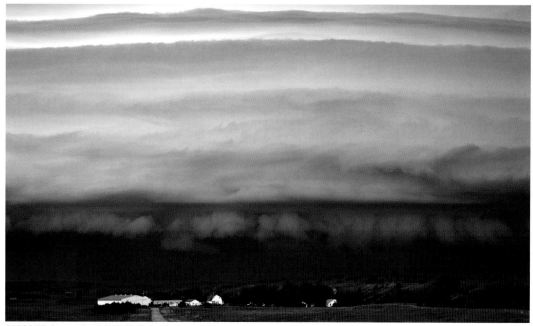

OPPOSITE: Supercell ABOVE: Shelf cloud

where it reaches -40° Celsius (which equals -40° Fahrenheit). In between these two levels, condensed water in the cloud can be *supercooled* - it is below 0° Celsius, but it remains in the liquid state. Supercooled water will freeze instantly when it encounters an ice particle, so it can freeze readily on a growing hailstone. But if the particle is too large to be held aloft by the updraft, it will simply fall out through the growth zone and cannot become very large. How fast does a hailstone fall? A stone the size of a baseball falls at more than 100 mph - about the speed at which a major league fastball pitcher can throw a fastball - which means that is roughly how strong an updraft has to be to produce a hailstone the size of a baseball (2¾ inches [7 cm] in diameter).

Not all intense updrafts produce large hailstones, for reasons that are not understood, but all hailstones are produced by strong updrafts (see also page 96).

Windstorms

Severe non-tornadic winds at the surface are almost always produced by strong downdrafts. Strong downdrafts, sometimes called *downbursts*, are produced by negative buoyancy (cold air sinking) or by the drag of heavy rainfall, or both. The gust fronts at the leading edge of the outflows produced by strong downdrafts are often marked by lines of low clouds, called *arcus* clouds, which also are called *shelf* clouds by many storm chasers. As shown in this book, these can take numerous forms.

Sometimes they have many layers – this layering results from vertical variations in humidity within the inflow air that is being forced upward by the gust front at the leading edge of the outflow. Outflow spreads out beneath a downdraft like pancake batter poured on a griddle, increasing the area affected so long as the downdraft continues. The winds produced by outflow are generally strongest when the gust front is near the downdraft. With multiple cells near each other, their outflows can merge, producing a large region of cool outflow.

Tornadoes

Tornadoes are most often associated with supercell thunderstorms. A rotating thunderstorm happens when thunderstorms develop in conditions where there is strong *vertical wind shear*. Vertical wind shear occurs when the wind changes its speed and/or direction with height. Although this situation can arise in many different ways, by far the most common instance is when the storms occur in association with an extratropical cyclone (see page 178), as a result of the jet streams produced by the strong horizontal temperature differences between north and south. In such cases, not only do the wind speeds increase with height, but also winds change direction rapidly with height as well. For storms in the United States, southerly winds near the surface carry warm, very moist air that picked up its water vapor from evaporation over the warm waters of the tropical oceans and the Gulf of Mexico. Above this, dry air from the Rocky Mountains slides over this low-level moisture, carried by southwesterly winds above the surface. This dry air is warm where it slides over the moisture, but cools rapidly with height. Above this, the

winds continue to increase with height to the core of the jet stream at about 10 miles above the ground.

An environment with strong vertical wind shear, including strong directional turning of the wind at low levels, promotes the development of rotation about a vertical axis inside any thunderstorm developing within it. This rotation, called a *mesocyclone*, first develops thousands of feet above the surface and, under the right conditions, can spread upward and downward inside the thunderstorm, resulting in rotation of the entire storm from top to bottom. Such a thunderstorm has become a supercell thunderstorm and, although the process by which it occurs is not well understood, about 20% of supercells go on to produce tornadoes. The great majority of tornadoes are produced by supercell thunderstorms. Even when they don't produce tornadoes, most supercells (about 95%) produce some form of severe weather.

However, a few tornadoes develop from thunderstorms that do not have mesocyclones (i.e., they are not supercells). The process by which such tornadoes arise is not well understood, but is thought to be associated with pre-exiting small-scale rotation about a vertical axis in the environment of the developing thunderstorm.

Supercell Storms

A classic (CL) supercell has a visual appearance, under the right viewing conditions, like that illustrated in fig. 4. The area between the updraft and the precipitation area beneath the downstream anvil is sometimes called the *vault*. This might not be visible when the updraft is close to the precipitation falling from the anvil.

The whole storm is rotating and the *wall cloud* marks an area where the mesocyclone is drawing rain-cooled

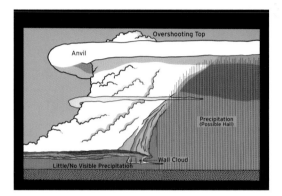

air from the downstream precipitation cascade into the updraft. Sometimes, as that rain-cooled air flows into the wall cloud, it is marked by a *tail cloud*. The wall cloud has a lowered cloud base because of the relatively high humidity of the air flowing inward from the precipitation area. When looking down on the storm from above (fig. 5), the precipitation cascade results in the so-called *forward flank downdraft* (FFD), while the *rear flank downdraft* (RFD) creates the so-called *clear slot* behind the wall cloud, causing the region of updraft to become curved into a horseshoe shape. Updrafts develop along the gust front associated with the RFD, rising into the storm along the *flanking line* of updraft curving into the mesocyclone.

Supercells can take on other forms, depending on how much precipitation is occurring within the mesocyclone. The *low precipitation* (or LP) supercell is illustrated schematically in fig. 6. In general, such storms produce little or no rainfall, but there can be large hail

Fig. 4: Schematic view of a classic supercell, looking toward an approaching storm. The storm is moving from left to right, extending beyond the edge of the illustration.

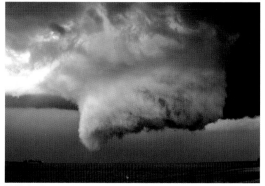
Wall cloud

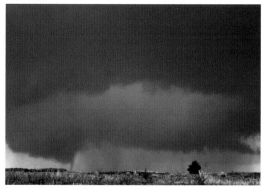
Rear flank downdraft

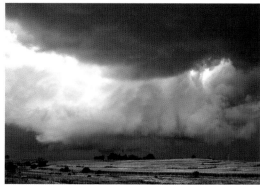
RFD, shot from the back

falling near the mesocyclone. LP supercells tend to be smaller than CL supercells and are much less likely to become tornadic. Because there is relatively little rainfall to evaporate, they do not generally produce much in the way of strong "straight-line" wind. Such storms are most commonly seen in the Great Plains of the United States.

At the other end of the supercell spectrum is the *high precipitation* (HP) supercell, shown schematically in fig. 7. HP supercells have considerable rainfall wrapped around their mesocyclones, falling within the RFD area. Therefore, the "clear slot" region is not clear at all – instead, it is filled with rain, and possibly hail. On some occasions, a so-called "beaver's tail" is seen extending from the general storm base along the gust front marking the FFD precipitation area. This is not the same as the tail cloud, which is tied to the lowered cloud base of the wall cloud. On some occasions, even a CL supercell can have a beaver's tail, but they are most commonly seen with HP supercells. Obviously, HP supercells can produce heavy rainfall, and often produce giant hail, very strong outflow winds, and tornadoes. The HP form of supercell is probably the most commonly observed supercell. It is common for supercells to evolve into squall lines, but the reverse evolution – a squall line changing into supercells – is rare.

Fig. 5: Looking downward on the same storm as that illustrated in fig. 4. The view in fig. 4 is from the right of this schematic, and the storm is moving toward the upper right corner of the figure. Shading indicates what a radar would see. Gust fronts are shown by frontal symbols along the black lines.

Fig. 6: Schematic illustration of the visual appearance of an LP supercell.

Fig. 7: Schematic illustration of an HP supercell. The "inflow band" is known as a "beaver's tail" cloud formation.

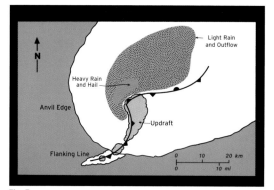
Fig. 5

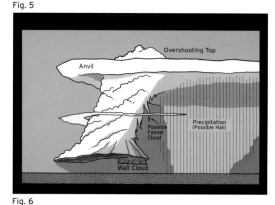
Fig. 6

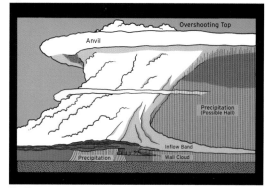
Fig. 7

Squall Line Storms

Thunderstorms are frequently organized into squall lines because the merged outflows often serve to develop new thunderstorms along the leading edge gust front. At times, there can be squall lines many hundreds of miles long. Squall lines may or may not be severe, and the conditions in which they become severe are similar to the conditions that produce supercells – the presence of strong vertical wind shear is generally favorable for severe squall lines to develop. Visually, squall lines are often marked by the so-called shelf cloud along the leading edge of the gust front. As noted earlier, these can appear to be layered in complex ways. It is not easy to gauge the intensity of the weather associated with a gust front just by its appearance – a very menacing-looking shelf cloud might not produce much more than brief heavy rain and a moderate gust of wind. When the gust front from the outflow moves well away from the precipitation, strong winds can sometimes pass over very dry ground, producing a dust storm (known as a *haboob*) as the outflow becomes filled with dust. Such dust storms are relatively common in deserts and semi-arid country around the world.

TORNADOES

Tornadoes develop mostly from beneath or near the wall cloud, but sometimes they can occur in other locations along the horseshoe-shaped updraft. On some occasions, the wall cloud may not be very evident as a lowering, but strong rotation of the cloud base will be visible. Occasionally, a tornado can change its appearance dramatically, perhaps several times. It may expand and shrink more than once, or it can evolve back and forth between single and multiple vortex structures.

Most tornadoes go through a distinct lifecycle, beginning with the *organizing stage*, during which a funnel cloud may (or may not) be present. Strong rotation will be seen in association with the wall cloud (if one is visible), but no debris cloud is present because the winds in the developing tornado are still not strong enough at the surface to cause dust and debris to be stirred up.

Note that the tornado is the wind, not the cloud, so even when the funnel cloud does not extend all the way to the ground, there may still be a tornado present. Some tornadoes have no funnel cloud at all, and the only way they can be detected by eye (or camera) is by their surface debris cloud and the strong rotation at cloud base above that debris cloud.

Next, the tornado enters the *mature* stage, when winds near the surface become strong enough to cause damage. The tornado funnel typically expands in size during this stage, or it might evolve into a *multiple vortex* form, with several funnel clouds forming and rotating about a common center. The funnel cloud associated with a tornado can appear very smooth (or laminar) or it can be ragged and turbulent, perhaps with embedded multiple vortices. The reasons for this are not entirely understood, but are likely to be related to different wind distributions within the tornado – not all tornadoes are the same. In some instances, the funnel cloud may never reach all the way to the surface, or it might only do so during the end of the tornado's lifecycle. Most commonly, however, the funnel extends all the way to the ground during the mature stage.

After this, the tornado enters the *shrinking* stage, which is obviously associated with a decrease in the diameter of the funnel cloud. Sometimes this stage is quite brief and in other tornadoes the shrinking stage can be rather prolonged. The funnel cloud might "retract" during the shrinking stage, although the continuing debris cloud will be evidence that the tornado is still ongoing.

Finally, the tornado enters the *dissipating* stage. Most commonly, this is marked by the evolution of the funnel cloud into a narrow, rope-like appearance and the spreading-out of the surface debris cloud. During this stage, the tornado is still capable of doing intense damage at the surface. Often, the funnel cloud becomes more and more contorted and may form loops just before the tornado decays. The funnel can also break up into segments that appear to be unconnected – remember that the tornado is the wind, not the cloud, so this appearance is deceptive. The segments remain part of a continuous vortex.

Not all tornadoes follow this lifecycle exactly. There are many variations of this basic evolution, but it is representative of what you will typically see.

Not all tornadoes occur with supercell storms. Sometimes, for reasons that are not completely understood, tornadoes develop in non-supercell storms. In a few instances, there may be several such tornadoes ongoing at the same time. The type of tornado that occurs commonly as waterspouts in the tropics and subtropical regions along coastlines may not be associated with thunderstorms at all – merely towering cumulus clouds. This same process can occur over land and can produce multiple tornadoes in the same way that waterspouts often develop in clusters. It is thought that this type of tornado forms along wind convergence boundaries when weak rotation over a radius of several miles develops along those boundaries as a result of *horizontal* wind shear – variation of wind speed and direction in the horizontal across the boundary. This rotation is then concentrated by the developing updrafts in the towering cumulus, forming tornadoes.

Tornadoes can also occur with squall lines, again for reasons that are not well understood. This should be distinguished from cases involving supercells embedded within squall lines, which while not common, are sometimes observed. The tornadoes developing in squall lines are thought to occur when strong horizontal shear is produced by intense outflow "jets" that cause the squall line to develop a bow-shaped structure. This creates regions of rotation about a vertical axis alongside the outflow jets that can become concentrated by updrafts into tornadoes.

The appearance of a tornado is strongly influenced by the surface characteristics over which it is passing, and by the lighting on it. When a tornado passes over dusty ground, it can be mostly or even completely shrouded in dust. On the other hand, it might pass over a surface with little or nothing to pick up, so it might have little or no debris cloud at all. If the air near the surface is humid, the development of a funnel cloud all the way to the ground is more likely than when the surface air has low relative humidity.

A funnel cloud is the same as any other cloud – it is formed by tiny droplets of condensed water vapor. Like any other cloud, a funnel cloud's appearance depends on the viewing angle and the background. When the background is dark, the tornado is seen as white if it is in direct sunlight, or a bluish grey when the illuminating light is diffuse skylight rather than direct sun. If the tornado is seen against the bright sky, it can appear black or a very dark grey, as it is being silhouetted. Late in the day, if the tornado is illuminated by the setting sun, it can be yellowish-golden or even blood red. People viewing the same tornado at the same time but from different directions can see it very differently.

CONCLUSION

As described in this brief summary of the science of storms, it is indeed possible to glean information about storms simply by seeing them. Their visible structure and evolution can reveal the processes going on within them which, in turn, allows a knowledgeable viewer to make some educated guesses about the weather they might produce. Responsible storm chasers such as Mike and Eric have actually contributed to the science of severe storms by sharing their still and video images with scientists and to the application of that science by weather forecasters. There is still much to learn about storms, but storm chasing has already improved our understanding and our ability to make forecasts and warnings that have considerable value in reducing casualties when severe storms affect populated areas.

Fig. 1: NOAA satellite image, courtesy of the National Center for Atmospheric Research, Research Applications Laboratory.
Fig. 2: Courtesy of the National Center for Atmospheric Research, Research Applications Laboratory.
Fig. 3: Drawings by the author, first published in C. A. Doswell, III, "Severe Convective Storms– An overview," *Meteorological Monographs* (American Meteorological Society), volume 28, no. 50, 2001, pp. 1-26.
Figs 4, 5 , 6, and 7: Drawings by the author and Joan Kimpel, first published in a NOAA storm spotter slide series.

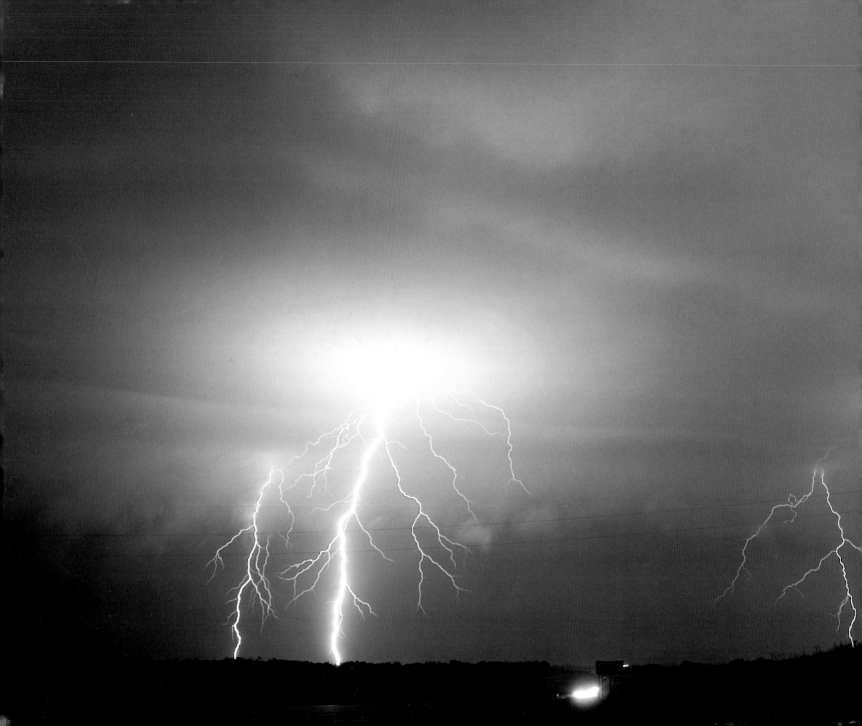

GLOSSARY
PHOTOGRAPHIC CREDITS
ACKNOWLEDGMENTS

GLOSSARY

anvil The flat, spreading top of a cumulonimbus cloud, often shaped like an anvil.

arcus cloud Low, horizontal cloud formation, e.g., roll clouds and shelf clouds, associated with the gust front.

beaver's tail A particular type of inflow band with a relatively broad, flat appearance suggestive of a beaver's tail. It is attached to a supercell's general updraft and is oriented roughly parallel to the pseudo-warm front, i.e., usually east to west or southeast to northwest. As with any inflow band, cloud elements move toward the updraft, i.e., toward the west or northwest. Its size and shape change as the strength of the inflow changes.

CG Cloud-to-Ground lightning flash.

coalescence When water droplets in a cloud collide and form raindrops.

convection Generally, transport of heat and moisture by the movement of a fluid. In meteorology, the term is used specifically to describe vertical transport of heat and moisture, especially by updrafts and downdrafts in an unstable atmosphere. The terms "convection" and "thunderstorms" are often used interchangeably, although thunderstorms are only one form of convection.

cumulus clouds Clouds that form at the top of thermals rising from near the surface in fair weather conditions: just high enough to produce condensation, but not unstable enough to develop into storms.

downdraft A small-scale column of air that rapidly sinks toward the ground, usually accompanied by precipitation as in a shower or thunderstorm.

dry line A boundary separating moist and dry air masses, and an important factor in severe weather frequency in the Great Plains. It typically lies north-south across the central and southern high Plains states during the spring and early summer, where it separates moist air from the Gulf of Mexico (to the east) and dry desert air from the southwestern states (to the west). The dry line typically advances eastward during the afternoon and retreats westward at night.

dry punch A surge of drier air; normally a synoptic-scale or mesoscale process. A dry punch at the surface results in a dry line bulge. A dry punch aloft above an area of moist air at low levels often increases the potential for severe weather.

equilibrium level (EL) The level at which a rising parcel that has been warmer than the environmental temperature at levels below becomes equal to the environmental temperature.

extratropical cyclone (ETC) A synoptic-scale cyclone (its horizontal extent is around several thousand kilometers) that typically contains warm and cold fronts with poleward, and equatorward moving airstreams, respectively.

forward flank downdraft (FFD) The region downstream, relative to the upper-level wind, where precipitation falls from the storm anvil, typically ahead of the mesocyclone, as distinct from the rear flank downdraft (RFD).

gust front The leading edge of gusty surface winds from thunderstorm downdrafts; sometimes associated with a shelf cloud or roll cloud.

instability The tendency for air parcels to accelerate when they are displaced from their original position: especially, the tendency to accelerate upward after being lifted. Instability is a prerequisite for severe weather - the greater the instability, the greater the potential for severe thunderstorms.

landspout A tornado that is not associated with a mesocyclone.

low precipitation storm or low precipitation supercell (LP) A supercell thunderstorm characterized by a relative lack of visible precipitation. Visually similar to a classic supercell, except without the heavy precipitation core. LP storms often exhibit a striking visual appearance; the main tower is often bell shaped, with a corkscrew appearance suggesting rotation. They are capable of producing tornadoes and very large hail. Radar identification is often difficult relative to other types of supercells, so visual reports are very important. LP storms almost always occur on or near the dry line, and thus are sometimes referred to as dry-line storms.

mammatus Rounded, smooth, sack-like protrusions hanging from the underside of a cloud (usually a thunderstorm anvil).

mesocyclone A storm-scale region of rotation, typically around two to six miles in diameter and often found in the right rear flank of a supercell (or